ALIVE
AT WORK

The Neuroscience of Helping
Your People Love What They Do

ALIVE
AT WORK

DANIEL M. CABLE

HARVARD BUSINESS REVIEW PRESS

Boston, Massachusetts

Library of Congress cataloging-in-publication information is forthcoming.

ISBN: 978-1-63369-425-5
eISBN: 978-1-63369-426-2

The paper used in this publication meets the requirements of the American National Standard for Permanence of Paper for Publications and Documents in Libraries and Archives Z39.48-1992.

to Daisy and Violet

CONTENTS

PART I
The Seeking System

Introduction: Our Organizations Are Letting Us Down   3

1. The Way Things Ought to Be   11

2. The Way Things Are—and How to Make Them Better   29

PART II
Self-Expression

3. Encouraging People to Bring Their Best Selves to Work   53

4. Promoting Self-Expression   67

PART III
Experimentation

5. Encouraging Serious Play   83

6. Expanding on Freedom and Creativity   97

7. Humble Leadership and Employees' Seeking Systems   115

Contents

PART IV
Purpose

8. Helping Employees Experience the Impact of Their Work   139

9. Crafting Narratives about Purpose   153

Notes   *175*

Index   *187*

Acknowledgments   *201*

About the Author   *203*

PART 1

THE SEEKING
SYSTEM

INTRODUCTION

OUR ORGANIZATIONS ARE LETTING US DOWN

"I wonder what my soul does all day when I'm at work."

—*Graffiti seen in London*

Let's start with a couple of questions. Are you excited about your work? Or does work make you feel like you need to "shut off" in order to get through it?

If you answered "yes" to the first question, you're in the fortunate minority. But, if you're in a position to lead and motivate others, there's still a good chance that those who fall under your leadership would answer no.

According to both US and global Gallup polls, about 80 percent of workers don't feel that they can be their best at work, and

70 percent are not engaged at work. What this means is that an overwhelming majority of the workforce is not "involved in, enthusiastic about, and committed to their work." And 17 percent of that group are "actively" disengaged: they are repelled by what they do all day.[1] Another recent study shows that over 87 percent of America's workforce is not able to contribute to their full potential because they don't have passion for their work.[2]

These numbers are alarming but, sadly, they're probably not surprising to you. I think all leaders know in their guts that engagement is an issue. Why? For one, we've all struggled with it ourselves. As a friend told me recently, "Sure, work sucks . . . that's why they call it work." At one point or other, we've all felt dulled by what we do at work—bored and creatively bankrupt. We've sometimes lost our zest for our jobs and accepted working as a sort of long commute to the weekend.

Yet even though we've all been there, it can be frustrating when our people aren't living up to their potential. It's exasperating when employees are disengaged and don't seem to view their work as meaningful.

It can be hard to remember that employees don't usually succumb to these negative responses for a lack of trying. They *want* to feel motivated. They *seek* meaning from their jobs. But some realities of organizational life are preventing them from feeling alive at work.

Here's a real-life example. When Tom started his gig after college designing and maintaining the website of a Big 4 accounting firm, he was excited. The pay was great, much better than the other two offers he had received, and he was told that there were lots of opportunities for personal growth.

The honeymoon didn't last long. As Tom recalled: "I soon found out my supervisor had no time or patience for experimenting. He was more concerned with protocol than personal development. It's like he's afraid of me trying new things because it might not go exactly as planned. It doesn't exactly leave much room for learning."

At first, Tom wasn't deterred. He tried to keep an open mind and optimistic attitude. He worked to improve some processes and inject some personality into his work, which gave him boosts of confidence. Unfortunately, Tom's boss was under pressure to meet website performance metrics, so she didn't have the flexibility to implement Tom's ideas.

Tom began to shut off. He did his work and completed his tasks, but he was becoming disengaged and unmotivated. He felt he was performing a series of scripted actions. Worse, he felt as if his boss wasn't responding to his creative impulses. After a year, Tom's tasks began to feel routine, small, and disconnected from a bigger picture.

Which is a shame. It's not as though Tom was a subpar performer who was only working for a paycheck. He was smart and talented, and he wanted to learn new things and expand his horizons. But his boss, he thought, was holding him back. So instead of contributing more to his employer, Tom looked elsewhere for fulfilment. While at work, he started bidding on website management projects via a freelancing app, and took on new projects that he was excited about. The irony was that his freelance work wasn't much different from his day job. But since it allowed him more ownership and freedom, it felt more meaningful to him.

Unfortunately, Tom isn't an outlier: he's like most employees in big organizations. As the Gallup studies suggest, a majority of employees don't feel they can be their best selves at work. They don't feel they can leverage their unique skills or find a sense of purpose in what they do. Most organizations aren't tapping into their employees' full potential, resulting in workplace malaise and dull performance.

Organizations are letting down their employees. We can do a much better job at maintaining their engagement with their work. But first, we need to understand that employees' lack of engagement isn't really a motivational problem. It's a biological one.

Here's the thing: many organizations are deactivating the part of employees' brains called the *seeking system*.[3] Our seeking systems create the natural impulse to explore our worlds, learn about our environments, and extract meaning from our circumstances.[4] When we follow the urges of our seeking system, it releases dopamine—a neurotransmitter linked to motivation and pleasure—that makes us want to explore more.[5]

The seeking system is the part of the brain that encouraged our ancestors to explore beyond Africa. And that pushes us to pursue hobbies until the crack of dawn and seek out new skills and ideas just because they interest us. The seeking system is why animals in captivity prefer to search for their food rather than have it delivered to them.[6] When our seeking system is activated, we feel more motivated, purposeful, and zestful. We feel more *alive*.[7]

Exploring, experimenting, learning: this is the way we're designed to live. And work, too. The problem is that our organizations weren't designed to take advantage of people's seeking systems. Thanks to the Industrial Revolution—when modern management was conceived—organizations were purposely designed to *suppress* our natural impulses to learn and explore.

Think about it: in order to scale up organizations in the late 1800s, our species invented bureaucracy and management practices so that thousands of people could be "controlled" through measurement and monitoring. Because managers needed employees to focus on narrow tasks, they created policies that stifled employees' desires to explore and try new things. These rules increased production and reliability, but reduced employees' self-expression, ability to experiment and learn, and connection with the final product.

Unfortunately, many remnants of Industrial Revolution management still remain. In an overzealous quest to be competitive, ensure quality, and comply with regulations, most large organizations have designed work environments that make it difficult for employees to experiment, stretch beyond their specialized roles, leverage their unique skills, or see the ultimate impact of their work. Most leaders today don't *personally* believe that people work best under these conditions. But each generation of managers walks into organizations where there are deeply entrenched assumptions and policies about control through standardized performance metrics, incentives and punishments, promotion tournaments, and so on. As a result, organizations deactivate their employees' seeking systems and activate their fear systems, which narrows their perception and encourages their submission.[8]

When people work under these conditions, they become cautious, anxious, and wary. They wish they could feel "lit up" and creative, but everything starts to feel like a hassle. They start to experience depressive symptoms: for example, a lot of headaches or trouble waking up and getting going in the morning.[9] Over time, they begin to believe that their current state is unchangeable, and they disengage from work.

But get this: our evolutionary tendency to disengage from tedious activities isn't a bug in our mental makeup—it's a *feature*. It's our body's way of telling us that we were designed do better things. To keep exploring and learning. This is our biology—it is part of our adaptive unconscious to know that our human potential is being wasted, that we are wasting away.[10] Jaak Panksepp, the late pioneer of affective neuroscience, said it best: "When the seeking systems are not active, human aspirations remain frozen in an endless winter of discontent."[11]

During the Industrial Revolution, limiting workers' seeking systems was intentional. Scientific management was considered rational and efficient because it helped ensure employees did only what they were told to do.

Things are different now. Organizations are facing the highest levels of change and competition ever, and the pace of change is increasing each year. Now more than ever, organizations need employees to innovate. They need employees' insights about what customers want. They need new ways of working based on technology that employees understand better than leaders. They need employees' creativity and enthusiasm in order to survive, adapt, and grow. They need to activate their employees' seeking systems.

I know this is possible. I've studied organizations as a professor and a consultant, and I have seen firsthand how they can work better. Throughout this book, we'll look at leaders across the world who have improved business outcomes while also improving the lives of employees by activating their seeking systems. We'll look at call centers in India, manufacturing plants in Russia, assembly facilities in Italy, nonprofits in the United States, delivery companies in the United Kingdom, airlines in the Netherlands, and banks in China. We will see again and again there are ways to activate the potential that lies dormant within all of us.

And it doesn't take a massive overhaul of a company's structure to make it happen. With small but consequential nudges and interventions from leaders, it's possible to activate employees' seeking systems by encouraging them to play to their strengths, experiment, and feel a sense of purpose.

Here's the plan for the book.

First, we'll take a closer look at the ins and outs of the seeking system: how it works and why it is needed to improve performance and help people live lives that are more worth living. The more you know about the mechanisms driving employee zest, motivation, and creativity, the better you'll be at increasing engagement and innovation.

Next, we'll look at why and how organizations are activating employees' fear systems and deactivating their seeking systems, and we'll examine ways to change this and help employees find "freedom" within the "frames" of their jobs.

From there, we'll tackle each trigger that activates the seeking system—self-expression, experimentation, and personalized purpose—and learn how leaders at all levels can increase employee zest and engagement through these triggers. You'll gain a more substantial understanding of why people love what they do—or more often, *don't* love what they do.

Most of all, you'll get an in-depth look at how employees think and feel about their work, and you'll discover ways to tap into their full potential. Activating the seeking system is like putting a plug into a live socket. The potential is already flowing right under the surface—you just need to access it to get employees lit up.

Here's the best part: it may sound crazy, but finding ways to trigger employees' seeking systems will do more than increase the enthusiasm, motivation, and innovation capabilities of your team. By improving people's lives, your *own* work as a leader will become more meaningful, activating your own seeking system. Things will work better for *you*. As Terri Funk Graham said, "The more passion people have for the work that they do, the more likely they are to demonstrate positive energy and success in life."[12]

Let's get started.

CHAPTER 1

—————

THE WAY THINGS OUGHT TO BE

Bonnie Nardi wasn't a gamer, and she couldn't understand how her son and students could spend hours of their lives sitting in front of screens. But after one of her anthropology students did a presentation on *World of Warcraft,* her interest was piqued. As someone who studied social life on the internet, she thought she could learn something from it. So she decided to give the massively popular role-playing game a try . . . you know, for research.

It didn't take long for Nardi to get what all the buzz was about. "Once I got over my initial disorientation in the game," she writes in *My Life as Night Elf Priest,* "I developed a strong sensation that I had woken up inside an animated fairy tale."[1] She was hooked.

In her book, Nardi details one of the first raids she participated in with a guild of fellow gamers she met online. Their mission: to obtain treasure by defeating a succession of evil "bosses," or monsters, who have special skills and powers that are extraordinarily difficult to defend against.

Anticipation was high.

5:30 p.m.

Although they are physically located around the globe, Nardi and her guildmates meet up a half-hour before their quest and chat via text and voice and share information that they've learned via wikis, blogs, and YouTube videos.

6 p.m. sharp.

The raid begins.

Nardi and her fellow guild members walk through a waterfall and take an elevator to reach a cavern below. She notes: "I have read about the elevator in player descriptions . . . and step carefully to wait for it to rise to our level." The guild enters the cavern and are met by a group of guards, or a trash mob, who are protecting the bosses. The guild uses everything at their disposal—spells, skill enhancements, potions, you name it—but can't get past the mob. Everyone is wiped out.

The guild retreats to a graveyard and regroups. Soon after, they try again, using a different combination of attacks and manage to defeat the guards before proceeding to battle the Lurker Below, a monster that must be fished out of the sea. "Things are going pretty well until the Lurker issues a 'spout,' during which we are supposed to dive off the platforms into the water," Nardi recalls. "Some dive too late and are killed. We try to keep going with a diminished raid but lack the resources to bring down Lurker."

The guild wipes out again and debriefs their experience over voice chat. The leaders of the raid offer encouragement and suggest improvements and new strategies to the team.

They fail again, but with each try they are learning more about the Lurker's techniques and movements until finally they're able to coordinate a successful attack.

Everyone celebrates. As Nardi describes it: "Through teamwork and personal skill, we have survived the Lurker's deadly spouts, geysers, and water bolts—or at least most of us have. The fallen are raised by the healers. A group screenshot is taken of us surrounding the dead Lurker and will be posted later to the Scarlet Raven website."

The guild continues on as the adventures unfold, venturing further into Serpentshrine Cavern and fighting Hydross the Unstable and other formidable bosses. It's an exhilarating process of trial-and-error, of learning and experimenting, of wiping out and succeeding.[2]

The raid winds down and Nardi logs off. Tired but amped up, she looks at the clock for the first time since they started.

10 p.m.

She's been playing for four and a half hours.

The Seeking System in Action

With their explorable worlds and open-ended outcomes, games such as *World of Warcraft* are catnip for our brains. Stories like Bonnie Nardi's offer us a glimpse at the seeking system in action.

13

Even though Nardi was playing in a virtual world, her positive emotions and her team's communication dynamics were real.

And the circumstances that evoked those feelings and dynamics can be replicated in other environments, too. I'm not talking about simple gamification of work here. It's not about keeping employees focused on simple, programmed behaviors through feedback and competition—I'm talking about improving people's enthusiasm toward experimentation, innovation, and learning.

We'll spend the rest of the book studying leaders who have enabled their employees to do exactly that. But before we dive into those examples, we should talk about what activates the seeking system, and what feelings and behaviors the seeking system evokes once it's been turned on.

Consider Bonnie Nardi. She didn't become hooked on *World of Warcraft* because of the cool graphics. That helped, for sure, but there was something else going on. She became hooked because it allowed her to express her unique skills as part of a team, explore new things, and find a sense of purpose—the three triggers that activate the seeking system.

Self-Expression

Like each of her guild members, Bonnie had a specific job to do. As a night priest, her superpower was to heal other players who had been wiped out during the action. She did this well. But even though she had a specific role, she was free to imagine it and interpret it any way she saw fit to help her team succeed. Bonnie was able to leverage her character's unique abilities and powers, which she had developed over a period of time and will continue to fine-tune in the future.

Experimentation

The game also featured a continual process of exploring and learning. As Nardi's guild progressed through the raid, they had to attempt difficult challenges repeatedly until they understood the environment better and found a blend of complementary skills, talents, and actions that allowed them to succeed. This approach fundamentally changed how they perceived and reacted to the world, and they became more flexible in their thinking. This is the agility, resilience, and willingness to experiment that most leaders today say they want in their employees, and that most employees would love to exhibit.[3] Most employees also would love it if their work swept them away for four and a half hours—the effect of dopamine—rather than forced them to watch the clock, wishing it would move faster.

Do you see how the game also normalized experimentation and exploration? It necessitated them, in fact. Although the chance of failure was high for each attempt, the cost was low and the lessons learned were immediate, personal, and emotional. This meant that Nardi and her guild could afford to think up new approaches and try them out, reacting according to how the environment responded to their previous ideas. Each subsequent experiment was based on better data, and they could continue to refine their strategy until it paid off.

Purpose

In combination, these circumstances gave Nardi an unexpected sense of purpose. It may sound surprising, but as we'll see later in this book, the feeling of purpose doesn't only come from curing diseases and improving the world. We'll learn how the feeling of purpose also ignites when we can see the cause and effect between our inputs and our team's progress. For example, sense of purpose soars when we can offer insights to our team about the environment and what might work better. Likewise, we feel a sense of purpose when we can experience firsthand how our unique role is necessary to other people. Because Nardi can see how her contributions help other players and allow the team to progress, playing *World of Warcraft* feels meaningful to her and so many others—even though it is "just a game."

Self-expression, experimentation, and a sense of purpose: these are the switches that light up our seeking systems.

The Benefits of the Seeking System

We still have so much to learn about our brains and how the electric impulses of neurons yield persistent experiences and emotions for us. Although it now seems clear that emotions and emotional behaviors are caused by neural activity, the evidence is not conclusive that all emotions are caused by architecturally and chemically distinct circuits in the brain.[4] Most neuroscientists agree, however, that one of the most basic emotional systems pertains to a functionally identifiable neural circuit that depends on dopamine, and that emotional system might be called interest, anticipation, or seeking.[5] This means that the seeking system is a real place in the brain: a neural network that runs between the prefrontal cortex and the ventral striatum. When activated with electrical impulses this system actually does "light up" in fMRI studies, showing the blood movement with the heightened activity. And, without even using electrical impulses, research on the seeking system holds great promise for leaders in organizations who want to prompt innovation and enthusiasm—and make life more worth living for their employees.

Jaak Panksepp described the seeking system this way: "These circuits appear to be major contributors to our feelings of engagement and excitement as we seek the material resources needed for bodily survival, and also when we pursue the cognitive interests that bring positive existential meaning into our lives."[6] (See figure 1-1.)

When we feel an urge to try new things and learn as much as possible about our environments, our seeking circuits are firing. This happens when we are curious or find something unexpected (like learning about the Lurker's spout, or watching how customers

FIGURE 1-1

The seeking system at work

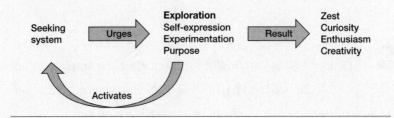

respond to our new social media campaign), or anticipate some-thing new (like riding the elevator behind the waterfall, or track-ing whether our team's new approach to manufacturing stops defects). As a result, we experience a jolt of dopamine, which feels pleasurable and can be thrilling. And since dopamine regulates our perception of time, we experience time differently, so that we might report that it seems to stand still even as it rushes by.[7] When the seeking system is activated, we experience "persistent feel-ings of interest, curiosity, sensation seeking, and in the presence of a sufficiently complex cortex, the search for higher meaning."[8]

This is a positive, invigorated feeling of anticipation that results in *zest*. According to Martin Seligman, a psychologist at the Uni-versity of Pennsylvania, zest leads people to live life with a sense of excitement, anticipation, and energy."[9] When we feel zestful, we see life or work as an adventure. And we approach new situations and changes with enthusiasm and excitement instead of appre-hension and anxiety.

The basic benefits of an activated seeking system are easy to see: when we're excited and follow our body's intrinsic urge to learn new things, the world feels like a better place to live, and we become more creative and productive.

And we perform better, too.

Performance

Do you know Journey's "Don't Stop Believing"—a staple at wed-dings and alcohol-soaked parties? But imagine you've been asked to sing this song, sober, in front of a complete stranger.

How do you think you'd do?

If you don't have any singing chops, you'd probably be anxious, nervous—maybe even fearful. Maybe you'd flub the words. Or would you?

Alison Wood Brooks, a professor at Harvard University, showed that the answer depends on whether you activate your positive emotions (like excitement) or negative emotions (like fear, which we discuss in chapter 2). In one study, Brooks recruited 113 people to sing Journey's hit in front of a stranger using Nintendo Wii's "Karaoke Revolution." But here's the catch: Brooks instructed half of the participants to say, "I am anxious" just before they sang. She instructed the other half to say "I am excited." One little word shouldn't matter, right?

As it turned out, people in the "excited" condition sang much better than the people who cued themselves to be anxious. Almost 30 percent better, jumping from 53 percent to 81 percent accuracy, as measured by Nintendo's voice-recognition software.[10]

Why? Either way, physiological arousal occurs in people who have to sing in front of a stranger. If we interpret this arousal as anxiety, the fear encumbers our enthusiasm and creativity (let's face it, fear is never going to help someone belt out a Journey song). When singers interpret their arousal as excitement, their seeking systems surge, causing them to be more playful, optimistic, and creative. If we can trigger our seeking system during stressful experiences, it promotes adaptive responses that "help shift negative stress states to more positive ones."[11]

Not so fast. After all, singing is one thing, because there ultimately is not a "right or wrong answer." And singing is based on vocal cords and posture, which obviously can be affected by physiological arousal. But what about math, where there *is* a right and a wrong answer?

Brooks studied this, too. Before a challenging math test, she told a different group of people, "You will complete a very difficult IQ test made up of eight questions under time pressure. For each question, you will have five seconds to select the correct answer. You will receive feedback about your accuracy after each question."

These instructions were custom-made to induce stress (research shows that the phrases *time pressure* and *IQ test* make people very anxious).[12] Participants were then randomly shown one of two instructions, displayed in large letters on their screens: "Try to remain calm" or "Try to get excited." Who got more of the difficult math questions correct: People who tried to calm down or people that tried to become more excited?

As you might have anticipated, participants in the "get excited" condition performed better, almost 8 percent better, on the same difficult math test. The difference between a B and a C grade.

As with the singing, positive emotions improve problem solving because people are better able to marshal their cognitive resources to cope with the task at hand, instead of being encumbered by fear and threat.[13] When people try to become calm under physiological arousal, on the other hand, they are telling themselves that the arousal is "bad"—that it is unwelcome. They code the same arousal as threat and anxiety, which activates fear, shuts down creativity, and hinders problem solving.

Brooks found the same phenomenon again in public speaking performances. Compared with participants assigned to say "I am calm," people assigned to say "I am excited" were perceived by independent judges as more persuasive, competent, confident, and persistent. This same phenomenon also has been found in a stream of sports psychology research: when athletes interpret their high arousal as excitement, they are more likely to exhibit playful, learning-oriented behaviors.[14]

This is why leaders need to know how to activate people's seeking systems. When you increase enthusiasm and excitement, you improve problem solving and creativity. This is how most people want to feel in their jobs—not only because these feelings lead to better work outcomes, but because we spend most of our waking hours at work, and positive emotions put more living into life.

Motivation

There are other benefits to the seeking system. Unlike the short-term motivation of extrinsic rewards such as financial bonuses, an activated seeking system has longer-term impacts on our motivation.

Picture a rat in a cage. On one side of the cage, the experimenter has placed lots of little trinkets that a foraging creature would love: sticks, corks, bottle caps, food pellets. The other side of the cage is bare. But this is no ordinary rat, because it has an electrode implanted in its seeking system. Researchers have rigged the rat up so that its seeking system is electrically stimulated only when it is on the side containing all the stuff.[15]

Based on what we have learned about the seeking system, what would we expect the outcome of this experiment to be?

a. The rat goes to the side with all the treasures and settles in.

b. The rat moves all of the treasures from the stimulation side to the nonstimulation side.

Let's work through this. If activating the seeking system created simple *hedonic* satisfaction—that is, pleasure sensations—then the rat should have gone over to the side with all the stuff and settled in, enjoying the pleasurable stimulation while sitting amid its treasures. Like a little furry despot.

But that's not what happened at all. In fact, after ten minutes, the researchers found that the rat had moved all the trinkets to the other side of the cage. Almost as if they had been trained, the rats had collected the items on the stimulation side and dropped them on the nonstimulation side.

An interesting finding, but what does it mean? It shows that the seeking system prompts an *intrinsic* urge to explore, rather than giving an *extrinsic* reward for an action.[16] When the seeking system is stimulated, an animal feels the urge to explore and investigate, to find whatever is potentially useful in the environment. In the rat experiment, when the seeking system was turned off (because the rat went to the nonstimulation side of the cage), it no longer felt this urge and dropped whatever it was carrying.[17] In the experiment, this meant that eventually all of the trinkets and items ended up on the nonstimulation side of the cage.

Does the seeking system work the same for humans? As Steve Cole, a professor of Medicine and Psychiatry and Biobehavioral Sciences in the UCLA School of Medicine, told me, "The seeking system doesn't seem to *reward* us for innovation and creativity, but rather it *drives and propels* those behaviors. The distinction is mainly temporal—reward happens after a behavioral event, whereas seeking happens before it. We are motivated to do a lot of things based on hope and aspiration that are not described by backward-looking rewards."

Why is this?

Professor Kent Berridge at the University of Michigan, who spent more than twenty years figuring out how the brain experiences pleasure, concluded that the mammalian brain has separate systems for what he calls *wanting* and *liking*.[18] Wanting is Berridge's terminology for the seeking system, whereas the liking system is the brain's reward center. When we experience the pleasure of a reward, it is the opioid system, rather than the dopamine system, that is being stimulated. These systems lead to very different effects: dopamine has an animating effect; opiates induce a happy stupor.[19]

This animating effect of the seeking system is optimal in work settings because it urges us into action instead of making us complacent. This is why Tom felt an urge to search for new freelance projects, and why Bonnie Nardi and millions of other gamers can play *World of Warcraft* for four hours straight. They "wanted" to explore and learn more and more.

Like a bottomless well that we just can't fill, our seeking systems are not placated after we've achieved a goal. In this sense, when the seeking system is paired up with a complex cortex, such as human beings possess, it also is related to Abraham Maslow's ideas about self-actualization: "Even if all these needs are satisfied, we may still often (if not always) expect that a new discontent and restlessness will soon develop, unless the individual is doing what he is fitted for. A musician must make music, an artist must paint, a poet must write, if he is to be ultimately happy. What a man can be, he must be. This need we may call self-actualization . . . the desire to become more and more what one is, to become everything that one is capable of becoming."[20]

So our seeking circuitry just won't rest, even when we have acquired the material possessions we lusted for. Even after we receive lots of extrinsic rewards and all our needs are fulfilled, our seeking systems still push us to find the best way to use our unique skills—and then do it.

This is the way we're meant to live. It's our biological imperative. Through evolution, we've retained our emotional impulses to explore, experiment, and learn.[21] Part of our brain urges us to learn new things and find new ways to use our unique skills, instead of performing monotonous generic tasks. And when we follow these urges of the seeking system, we get a dopamine release that not only feels good, it motivates us to explore more.

Happiness and Health

What it all comes down to is this: when we're working and living in environments where exploration and experimentation are encouraged, we're happier people.

And I'm not just talking about plain old happiness—*hedonic* well-being—which is defined as the pleasant feelings you experience when you get the things you want.[22] I mean *eudemonic* happiness, which refers to the meaning you feel in life.

What's the difference? Here's a quick quiz for you. Answer each question below using a number ranging from 1 ("never") to 6 ("always").

Over the last four months of your life, how often did you feel . . .

1. . . . happy? _____

2. . . . that your life has a sense of direction or meaning to it? _____

3. . . . satisfied? _____

4. . . . that you had something worthwhile to contribute to society? _____

Now, add up your answers to questions 1 and 3. If you scored above an 8, you might be happy to know that you are in the ninety-fifth percentile of hedonic happiness, compared with respondents in a recent study.[23]

But is "being happy" good for us? That is, is happiness biologically healthy? Our kneejerk answer might be yes, but actually it depends on how you answered questions 2 and 4. These questions get at the concept of purpose—our sense of meaning and direction in life, our involvement in something bigger than ourselves. It is a more purposeful happiness (scholars sometimes refer to this as *eudemonic well-being*). If you scored greater than 7 on these two items, you are above the ninety-fifth percentile in terms of purposeful happiness.

When it comes to your health, scoring high on both types of well-being is great.[24] But lots of people don't score high on both.

And four independent studies have revealed that it is far better for your immune system when you score high on purposeful happiness than hedonic happiness.[25] Unfortunately, less than a quarter of study participants were in that desirable situation.

In one study, Barbara Fredrickson (a psychology professor at the University of North Carolina) teamed up with UCLA's Steve Cole and asked eighty adults to respond to the same questions you answered above. The researchers then took blood samples and studied the functioning of their immune cells. They found that a high score of purposeful happiness was correlated with higher immunity (much more than hedonic happiness was correlated with immunity). In fact, the data revealed that people who are happy but have little sense of meaning in their lives have the same gene expression patterns as people who are enduring bad things in their lives. According to Fredrickson, "Empty positive emotions are about as good for you for as adversity."[26] Amazing.

This is where our seeking systems fit in. That circuit in our brains provides an intrinsic impulse for us to keep exploring our environments, learning, and finding meaning. "Empty" happiness characterizes a relatively shallow, self-absorbed life. Things go well, and our needs and desires are easily satisfied.[27] But our seeking systems are switched off.

Philosopher Aristotle clearly rejected this view of hedonic happiness. He said, "The many, the most vulgar, seemingly conceive the good and happiness as pleasure, and hence they also like the life of gratification. Here they appear completely slavish, since the life they decide on is a life for grazing animals."[28]

Unhealthy grazing animals, apparently.

The seeking system offers a biological way to understand and predict *exciting* and *purposeful* activities and feelings outside the realm that is normally thought of as rewarding in a *pleasurable* or *hedonic* sense. And the science suggests that this is important when it comes to cellular functioning and health.

Derren Brown, in his excellent book *Happy*, describes the Greek Stoic philosophers' viewpoint on virtue: "Deciding the virtue of a person or thing comes from first understanding what that thing's unique quality or purpose is in the world, and then seeing if it is doing *that* as well as possible."[29] Maybe, for us humans, this is what the seeking system is urging us to do: to explore our environments in order to discover our personal potential in the world, and then express ourselves in that way. Following our seeking system's urges make us feel good in a purposeful way, which makes us healthier and happier.

In chapter 2, we are going to take a look at how things are in many jobs and organizations, and how those circumstances shut off people's seeking systems—resulting in worse health, low motivation, and poor engagement. But it's not all bad news—far from it. The rest of the book focuses on practical ways that leaders can overcome these organizational realities and ignite employees' seeking systems by encouraging them to craft more freedom into the frame of their jobs.

CHAPTER 2

THE WAY THINGS ARE—AND HOW TO MAKE THEM BETTER

Martin Seligman, renowned psychologist at the University of Pennsylvania, is an expert in happiness and optimism. But he didn't start his career studying positive psychology: he started out by shocking dogs.

When Seligman was in grad school, he would place a dog in a large crate that was divided by a small fence, which the dogs could see and jump over.[1] Mind you, this was not for giggles: he was writing a field-changing dissertation on learning. After placing a dog on one side of the crate, Seligman administered a painful shock through the floor that the dog was standing on.

What do you think happened?

Before you answer, you should know there were two types of dogs. One set of dogs was "naive." They had never experienced the painful shocks before. A second set of dogs had been part of a previous experiment, where they were placed in a "Pavlovian hammock" with holes for their legs to dangle free, and then given painful shocks on their feet. The dogs struggled to get away, but the hammock restrained them. They could neither avoid nor escape the shocks.

I know, that's pretty unkind. But it gets even worse. Sorry.

When the naive dogs were shocked, most of them howled and ran around and eventually jumped over the fence to escape.

But most of the dogs who had been previously shocked in the hammock did not jump over the fence. Instead, Seligman wrote, this set of dogs "sits and lies, quietly whining, until shock terminates."

Those "experienced" dogs had learned *helplessness*. From their previous conditioning exercise, they had learned to "give up and passively accept the shock" since there was nothing they could do about it. They learned to "take it" because their past experiences taught them that they were helpless.

Learned helplessness is a three-headed monster. It alters our emotional states (we grow resigned), lowers our motivation (we no longer even try), and changes our cognitive reasoning (we generalize our experience to other environments).[2] Learned helplessness often continues when we go from one situation to another, and it is reliably difficult to overcome once it sets in. Electrical shocks are not usually used on human subjects, as you might suspect. But, unfortunately, learned helplessness occurs in many settings.[3]

Especially work.

Many employees find themselves caught in a crossfire between their biological seeking systems and their organizational realities. Their built-in biology urges them to explore their environments, experiment and learn, and assign meaning. But most people work in organizations where they don't feel that it is possible to do any of these things. After a spate of bad experiences, such as being shut down for using creativity instead of following the rules, employees begin to ignore the urges of their seeking systems. This means they shut off the dopamine and let their anxieties dominate. Like the dogs in Seligman's experiment, many employees learn how to shut off and just "take it"—an attitude that results in disengagement at work and depressive symptoms in life. They end up making a living but not a life.

Organizational Realities

But wait a minute. Today's leaders *know* that employee engagement and creativity are needed for organizations to thrive. So why does it seem to employees as though leaders are trying their best to make them feel bored, unmotivated, and helpless? It doesn't seem to make sense. What are these organizational realities and where do they come from?

We need to remember that big organizations are relatively new things. We invented them about 150 years ago as a new means of producing stuff and increasing the scale of sales and distribution. The method worked well, in some ways. The assembly line, for example, allowed Henry Ford to lower costs and increase reliability, which democratized the automobile. Prices of an automobile fell from $850 in 1908 to less than $300.[4] This was done by following the principles of *scientific management*: breaking all the units of work up into small tasks, and then motivating people to become very proficient at these tasks, repeating them again and again very quickly. As Frederick Taylor urged: "The work of every workman is fully planned out by the management at least one day in advance, and each man receives in most cases complete written instructions, describing in detail the task which he is to accomplish, as well as the means to be used in doing the work."[5]

Controlling employees like this was a novel way of thinking at the time. Remember, before the existence of large organizations with thousands of employees, programmed work would not have been necessary. But scaling up production meant that managers needed a way to control the behaviors of employees (robotics and artificial intelligence were not even part of science fiction yet). Look up the definition of management: "controlling things or people."[6] Bureaucracy and management were the solutions invented to solve the problem of controlling thousands of employees.

The problem was that each employee had a seeking system. What in the world would motivate employees to do something repetitive and disconnected from a larger purpose when part of their brains are urging them to explore, experiment, and find meaning? It's time to talk about fear.

Fear Is Kryptonite to the Seeking System

Today we are born preloaded with emotions (for example, fear or curiosity) and corresponding action tendencies (for example, focusing on the threat or playing around) because they helped our ancestors survive. Let's take a dramatic case. If you are walking down a dark alley at night and someone suddenly comes running up fast behind you (even if it is your friend), your fear system kicks in and the amygdala (an almond-shaped organ in the center of your brain) sends signals to your autonomic nervous system.[7] Fear results in physical reactions. For example, your perception organs focus almost entirely on the threat, narrowing your attention and blocking out information not relevant to the threat. Adrenaline floods into your blood and wraps your muscles tighter to make you faster and stronger. You did not try to do this: your fear took matters into its own hands, so to speak, and acted based on hardwired tendencies.[8] Animals born without fear would not have survived long enough to have children, and that fearless branch of the animal kingdom would have been pruned.

Just as the fear system helped our ancestors survive, it is easy to see why an emotional system that motivates exploration and learning would support survival. Across the ages, nature did not always provide the necessary resources for survival. The seeking system is the motivational engine that each day gets mammals to venture out into the world, even though they don't know what they'll find.[9] On average, mammals whose brains motivated them to explore and learn about their environment were more likely to survive and have children.

But say there was a battle between our seeking systems and our fear systems. Which one would win?

For evolutionary reasons, fear will win. Check out this study, for example. When lab technicians put two young rats together, they almost always start to play—pouncing, chasing, and wrestling each other. The rats, that is, not the lab technicians. According to Jaak Panksepp, this spontaneous play is a robust finding, and we know it's play because of the rats' "laughter." Yes, rats laugh. I did not know this until I talked with Panksepp, but rats make measurable 50 kHz chirps when they are happy and excited. The rats' play is a form of experimenting, learning, and practice, as they explore their potential in terms of strength, agility, and dominance. To the best of our scientific knowledge, the basic urge to play exists among most mammals. Play is how we learn what we're capable of.

Panksepp describes an experiment in which he assessed rats' play (he measured both their laughter and their invitations to play, such as pouncing) before and after he placed a small tuft of cat fur in their play space.[10] The smell of the fur activated rats' innate fear system, and their play was completely inhibited. In the four days before they were exposed to the fur, the rats exhibited an average of fifty invitations to play in the five-minute sessions. After the introduction of the cat fur, play invitations dropped to zero (play invitations for the control group, which did not receive the fur, remained at fifty). It took three days after the fur was removed for the rats to slowly start to play again at all, and the levels of play never returned to the pre-fur sessions (thirty-five was the new high, even after five days with no fur).

What we are seeing here is the *inhibiting relationship* between the seeking system and the fear system. When one system is activated, the other shrinks back. This works like the accelerator and brakes on a car. The accelerator gets you places, but speed can be dangerous. The brakes keep you safe, but if you only use brakes you don't get anywhere. And, if you mash them both to the floor, the car doesn't move.[11]

The accelerator-brakes analogy fits the evidence about human emotions, because we know that negative emotions dominate positive emotions.[12] Losing money, being abandoned by friends, and receiving criticism all have a greater impact on people than winning money, gaining friends, and receiving praise. As Panksepp told me, in all species that have been studied, playfulness is inhibited by negative emotions such as fear.

Perfect for scientific management. After all, Frederick Taylor wanted employees to focus on following orders, not play around or experiment. So managers invented personnel policies that were very detailed in describing procedures and outcomes to be accomplished, by when. They set up careful measurements, and imposed punishments when specific expectations were not met (see figure 2-1). On the upside, fear-based management solved the problem of how to control so many employees when you couldn't know them or develop trust. On the downside, this became the root of employees' learned helplessness at work.

FIGURE 2-1

Scientific management at work

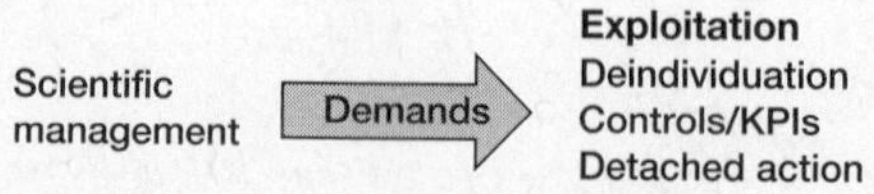

| Scientific management | Demands → | Exploitation
Deindividuation
Controls/KPIs
Detached action |

To be fair, when it was invented, scientific management was a viable way for an organization to be competitive. Entrepreneurs or senior leaders could find the most efficient methods of production and tell employees exactly what to do. Back before telephones, airplanes, or computers, information traveled a lot more slowly, and the environment changed less frequently. This meant that organizations had decades to exploit new approaches and inventions before they were copied.

For example, in 1913 Henry Ford wanted to "put the world on wheels" by bringing the elite automobile to the masses through the production of the largest number of cars for the lowest cost. He introduced the assembly line, and his company dominated the industry using this innovation for over a decade.

In case you haven't noticed, the speed of change has been accelerating. While the telephone took seventy-five years to reach 50 million users, TV took thirteen years, and the internet took only four years.[13] As environments change fast and faster, and innovations are copied more and more quickly, employer-imposed scripted and repetitive behaviors are no longer a way for leaders to gain a competitive advantage. Organizational survival today comes from employees being proactive—using creativity and ingenuity to solve problems without waiting for instruction. The most valuable employees think like owners and develop new approaches to solving problems, instead of waiting until management works out a full-blown solution and teaches them the new procedures.

The seeking system is built for this proactive approach, because it creates enthusiasm and curiosity. Dopamine doesn't just feel good, it makes employees into a "volunteer army" that begins change rather than resisting it.

The problem is that, even though the business landscape has changed dramatically, organizational policies haven't. And the bad effects of industrialization on the seeking system are still lingering. Here's how.

Limited Roles

The dream of scientific management was that employees' quirks and self-expression wouldn't get in the way of standardized processes. And so even today, in big organizations, most people work very specialized jobs. We're mechanics or web designers or salespeople or teachers and so on. Our employers designed the jobs and then found people who could perform the necessary behaviors. We have a set of predetermined tasks to accomplish in a certain amount of time.

This is, of course, much less true in small startups, where work routines are still being invented to solve problems. In startups, all employees are expected to use their best skills help the organization survive and grow—whether what they're doing is part of a formal job or not. But as a startup grows from a tight-knit group of fifty employees into an organization ten times that size, leaders realize they don't have the cognitive ability to really know or trust five hundred people.[14] The solution often is to tighten the frame of jobs by making behaviors more predefined. Careful measurement becomes a surrogate for trust.

Now, when employees start a new job or accept a new role in a big company, this isn't always a big problem. Everything seems new, and there's a lot to learn. A newcomer may not be expressing her unique skills, and may not even be clear how her small set of tasks fit into the bigger picture, but her seeking system is firing as she's figuring out the cause and effect of how things get done. Recall Tom, the web designer at a Big 4 firm we met in the introduction. Fresh out of college, he was idealistic and energetic, and he dove headfirst into his work. But, after a while, he tried to bring some of his own ideas to the job, and he was shot down. As the months turned into years, the work grew repetitive and tedious because he wasn't learning much, and he grew bored. The dopamine was missing and the days seemed to drag.

Tom's response is perfectly normal. His brain wasn't hardwired to thrive in a limiting role like this. During almost all of our evolution, humans lived in small tribes of fifty or so people. For most people, there was very little specialization—everybody in each tribe learned how to do most of the activities needed for survival, such as making clothes and finding food and shelter. Remember, we only very recently invented farming (twelve thousand years ago), which allowed us to leave the hunter-gathering existence behind. And the concept of money and payment is even more recent (about six thousand years old).[15] That's not very long ago in evolutionary terms. Even when we fast-forward to the 1700s and 1800s, there was nothing like the specialization that we see today. Sure, people were farmers, shopkeepers, and blacksmiths, but very few organizations except the military would have employed hundreds of people.

For example, in the 1800s, you would buy shoes made by a cobbler, who made a shoe for you from beginning to end: measuring your foot, cutting and sewing the leather, and negotiating the price.

So in the 1800s you could buy shoes from someone who performed multiple tasks, using multiple skills. There wasn't a Nike. There wasn't an organization of sixty-three thousand people selling shoes with a specific swoosh in every country to every family in the world. Instead of making bespoke shoes from beginning to end for a specific customer, most of the people who work in big companies are hyper-specialized on small, disconnected tasks. One person might be in charge of purchasing the mesh for running shoes, spending forty hours each week following specific processes to obtain materials she didn't choose, for shoes she didn't design, for customers she'll never meet. Another employee might manage and update the website with pictures he doesn't take, text he doesn't write, and prices he didn't set. And Nike is not a particularly large company: Accenture has 375,000 employees. Tata has 600,000. The China National Petroleum Corporation employs 1.6 million people. Walmart employs 2.1 million.

Most of the people in most of these companies work on pre-scripted, specialized tasks where there is not much room to use unique strengths or try new approaches. And we all know how it starts to feel once we've worked on the job for a while: these very specialized jobs can start to feel confined and repetitive. We notice, for example, that time starts to become a "problem" instead of a treasure. We feel that we want to get through the hours more quickly, but they seem to loom before us as we count down the hours or the minutes until our next break (so that we can check Facebook). Our seeking systems urge us to be curious and learn, but because of tight performance measurement and penalties, we can't exactly play around and try something new. When we get to this point of machine-like repetition with no new learning on the horizon, going to work can feel very aversive—as though it is not real life but just something to get through.

But it *is* real life. That's what's tragic for both organizations and employees. For organizations, it's terrible that employees are so disengaged from their work when they have the potential for energy and enthusiasm. For employees, it's terrible to have to wish their hours away rather than living them with meaning. Small sets of confined activities is why Yuval Noah Harari argues persuasively in his book *Sapiens* that our ancestors fifteen thousand years ago had it better than we do today.[16]

Controls and KPIs

Leaders need continuity and control. By this, I mean that they need to be sure that regulations are met and promises made to customers are kept. This is not evil, this is practical. You could even say that's why managers have their jobs, ever since the

Industrial Revolution. Since future changes and challenges are unclear, it often seems safer to have employees behave in pre-specified ways.

To increase managers' control back in the 1850s, Frederick Taylor helped them put careful measures in place to show whether or not employees have met expectations. This allowed managers to motivate workers by taking away income and status when they were not fulfilling their prescribed tasks. As we learned from the discussion above, fear of loss is very salient and threatening, which narrows employees' attention and focuses them on their specific tasks. Think about how it makes you feel when you will be punished unless you meet challenging, specific, expectations. Fine-tuned measurements that are tied to rewards and punishments allow organizations to direct employees and *exploit* the knowledge and processes that already are known to work.[17]

So far, so good, from an organizational control perspective.

"Good" unless the organization needs innovation and adaptability, that is. Because fine-tuned control that exploits existing processes makes it hard for workers to explore and experiment with new alternatives. By definition, the outcomes of experimenting and playing are "uncertain, distant and often negative."[18] Policies that make us anxious about losing pay, promotions, and status act like the cat fur: our fear system shuts off our seeking system. Biologically, this inhibits our creativity and desire to play. We just don't ever feel like there is enough time to explore if our behaviors and outcomes are all tightly mapped out in advance, with financial and career implications if we miss them. The frame of scientific management leaves our seeking systems very little chance (see figure 2-2 for the full picture).

FIGURE 2-2

Why disengagement dominates organizational life

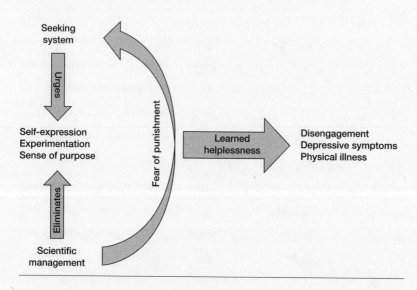

In an IBM poll of CEOs worldwide, creativity was identified as the single most important leadership trait for success.[19] So leaders these days *know* they need innovation. But in reality, they punish the behaviors that could lead to experimentation and innovation. By definition, experiments are unpredictable and often do not work to plan (which is, of course, exactly how experiments lead to learning). This is why it is easy for managers to dislike creativity when we are afraid of not hitting monthly revenue or weekly delivery targets.[20] Creative ideas must be both novel and practical, but the research shows that we often punish the novel and reward the practical.[21]

For example, psychologist and Wharton management professor Jennifer Mueller and her colleagues have discovered that people often reject creativity—even when they themselves espouse creativity as a desired goal. In one study, Mueller showed that when people experienced uncertainty, they displayed an unconscious negative bias toward creativity. The research calculated the strength of people's mental associations between creative words (for example, *inventive*) and positive words (*sunshine, laughter*) versus negative words (*agony, rotten*). Participants had to press one key in response to creativity + bad pairs (for example, *inventive* and *agony*) and press another key in response to creativity + good pairs (*inventive* and *sunshine*). People in uncertain situations were much quicker at judging when creativity was paired with negative words, showing how creativity is linked to negativity in our brains. In some ways this is not surprising—novel ideas can lead to ridicule, failure, and social rejection.[22] It's hard to be the first one to tell people that the earth is not the center of the universe. Or to tell senior leaders at Kodak that digital will eclipse film.

Moreover, our bias against creativity damages our ability to recognize creative ideas.[23] In another set of studies, Mueller and her colleagues demonstrated that when employees expressed creative ideas, it negatively affected whether they were viewed as having leadership potential—even though they were working in jobs that required creative problem solving!

So, the world is changing frequently and organizations need to adapt to survive, and leaders know they need employee innovation. However, it is very common for both control-oriented personnel policies and managers with unconscious biases to punish employees for creative ideas, or for trying innovations that don't satisfy pre-specified performance targets. Even though we may say we want employee creativity and innovation, we place even greater value on exploiting existing ideas and processes that are tried and true. This makes organizations "highly predictable and increasingly rigid."[24] As my friend and colleague Jules Goddard at

London Business School writes: "The language of planning and control, of targets and KPIs, of metrics and benchmarks, of efficiency and excellence, of specialisation and standardisation, of jobs and careers betrays a way of thinking that is wholly unsuited to the challenges confronting firms today."[25]

Most managers today can sense this. They know that the rituals of SMART goals and forced distributions of performance ratings don't inspire employees to try new approaches to solving problems. But they often feel like they have little other choice, since these assumptions and practices are deeply entrenched in the organizational culture: performance evaluation systems, pay systems, promotion systems, and so on. These systems of management today are essentially the same as they were a hundred years ago.[26]

Many of us accept that this is *the* way to set up organizations— almost as if it is a natural law, like gravity. Someone at the top figures out a best way to do things, breaks it into small boring pieces, and then uses a combination of fear and money to motivate us to do our work. It's not meaningful or exciting, but that's why they call it work, right?

This Industrial Revolution approach isn't only bad for our mental states; it's bad for our organizations. We can do much better.

Balancing the Freedom and the Frame

To be successful, can organizations just tell their employees to "Be free! Experiment! Do whatever you like!"? Although this is possible (Valve Software has racked up $3.5 billion doing exactly that[27]), organizations still need employees to meet regulations, deliver on promises to customers, and not "break" the organization. There needs to be a frame.

What we need to do is help employees find the freedom in that frame. The freedom refers to the space where employees can experiment, try new things, express themselves, and play to their strengths. Great organizations balance a strong sense of employee freedom and experimentation within an operational frame. Some leaders refer to this as working on the airplane while you're flying it. Of course, this is only possible when employees understand the big picture—the organizational frame—and the shared purpose of the work.

If we can get the tension right between the freedom and the frame, it not only activates employees' seeking systems but it directs their enthusiasm and ideas toward solving organizational problems. So work feels more like real life to employees, and organizations get the creativity and innovation that keeps them relevant. Too good to be true? No, that's just a solid win-win. Let's look at an example.

A Coalition of the Willing

Remember Eyjafjallajökull? The Icelandic volcano erupted in April 2010, resulting in a massive ash cloud that spread across Western and Northern Europe. Flights stalled for six days, stranding thousands of passengers. During this time, KLM and other airlines also experienced an eruption—customers' requests for information jammed their call centers. The overload blocked their ability to provide customer support when it was needed most.

To solve this problem, some KLM Royal Dutch Airlines employees decided to try something new. They provided service updates on Facebook and Twitter. It may sound obvious to us now, but these were the early days of social media. Twitter was only three years old at the time. Most organizations were not using social media to communicate with customers.[28]

And remember, KLM was no small startup. For more than ninety years, the airline has operated flights throughout the world. With more than thirty-two thousand employees serving more than 133 international destinations, KLM is one of the largest and most successful international airlines. And, the airline industry is *very* regulated—there are a lot of rules when you are moving people 500 miles per hour 30,000 feet above sea level. So you can imagine the frame for employees is fairly established, which could have thwarted creativity and innovation unless employees were encouraged to experiment. Add to this that there were no policies for communicating on these new social media platforms, and it certainly is conceivable that an employee would get something wrong.

At first, the freedom to use social media to communicate with customers paid off. It was a lemons-into-lemonade situation, because KLM received positive publicity during the crisis. In fact, Jeffrey Mann, a member of the Gartner Blog Network, wrote, "KLM shows how to use social media during ash crisis, and Air France shows how not to."[29]

But the airline's social media experiments did not always work exactly as planned. Of *course* they didn't; employees were still experimenting and learning with a new way of communicating. For example, the Netherlands beat Mexico during a World Cup match and emotions were running high. A KLM employee tweeted a picture of an airport departures sign under the heading "Adios Amigos." Next to the word "Departures" was a man with a moustache and sombrero. On the one hand, KLM got a lot of exposure— the post went viral, creating millions of social media movements. On the other hand, Mexican actor Gael Garcia Bernal tweeted to tell his 2 million–plus followers that he would never fly with KLM again, and hundreds of other people complained.[30]

KLM could have fired the employee and shut down its social media experimentation. Instead, the company apologized to the public, deleted the post, and tried to learn where the frame became broken. KLM spokeswoman Lisette Ebeling Koning explained, "It was meant to be a joke, but there was too much negative reaction." Marnix Fruitema, director general of KLM in North America, wrote, "In the best of sportsmanship, we offer our heartfelt apologies to those who have been offended by the comment."[31]

This outcome at KLM offered important learning about social media communications. Employees had the freedom to use their interests and strengths to contribute to the team, but they needed to learn how to use this freedom within the frame of customer commitments and legal regulations. Experimenting is essential to innovation and agility, but it is not possible to predict in advance all the places where the freedom will rub up against the frame.

So the airline encouraged employees to experiment with social media within the frame of normal operations. For example, a KLM leader at Schiphol Airport told me how a small group of flight attendants and other employees who were intrigued by social media were encouraged to experiment with a budget of €10,000. None of the employees *had* to do it; just those who were interested in helping. This self-selected team decided to first scour the internet for people who mentioned KLM in their tweets or Facebook posts, or who checked in using Foursquare. Then they developed ways to surprise these social media–savvy customers. Using people's profiles on Facebook, LinkedIn, and Twitter, the team found interesting facts about passengers to come up with creative, personalized surprises for them. Finally, the "surprise team" went all-out to locate these people before their flights left, to give them the personalized gifts.

For example, the team found out that Tobias Hootsen was on his way to Dubai indefinitely. So, they created a "homesick package," and tracked him down in the airport to present it to him. Another traveler, Willem van Hommel, tweeted that he would miss an important soccer game of his team because he was flying to New York. The KLM team surprised him with a Lonely Planet guide to the city with all soccer bars marked in blue to make sure he wouldn't miss the game. Another passenger going hiking in Rome received a sports watch that tracks distances and walking speed.[32]

This is how KLM balanced the freedom in the frame. Employees were not ordered to use social media, and the approach was not scripted by senior management. A small group of willing employees was given a small budget to experiment with social media, mostly to learn how its audience responds. KLM monitored how recipients reacted to their surprises—whether they tweeted about it or mentioned it on Facebook.[33] In this case, the forty gifts created a social media storm: the KLM Twitter feed was viewed more than one million times in three weeks. Not bad for an experiment based on something that the employees found intrinsically interesting and were excited to try. But leaders needed to have the strategy of encouraging freedom within the frame, and also needed to be ready to learn when the experiments did not go exactly as planned.

Together, KLM's experiments with social media have helped it stay connected to tech-savvy customers. KLM now has 150 social media customer service agents who generate $25 million in annual revenue, and the company is regularly voted as the most social-media-relevant airline.[34] KLM recently was recognized for its digital presence with six "Webby Awards"—known as the Oscars of the internet—along with Airbnb, the *New Yorker*, Lady Gaga, Google and the *Washington Post*.[35] The behaviors that led to this learning, and this relevance, were not pre-scripted by senior leaders: they were invented by employees with activated seeking systems.

Within an organizational frame, KLM encouraged self-expression, experimentation, and experiencing the impact of work. These are the triggers of the seeking system, which led to employee enthusiasm and creativity that helped the organization adapt and innovate.

As we move through the book, you will see how each of these triggers has implications for us, both as leaders of others and as employees ourselves. As we'll see, investing in these triggers causes employees to reconsider their work, because it helps people bring more living into their lives. And it doesn't take a lot to make this happen. We'll see leaders asking new hires to share stories about themselves on their first day, encouraging employees to make up their own job titles, offering "free time" to work on personalized projects, and finding ways for employees to experience the impact of their work on others. These can all activate the seeking system.

Investing in these triggers is the most important thing we can be thinking about. Of course, there will still be the "grind" of hard work, in the same way there is a lot of repetition in achieving physical fitness or being a competitive athlete. But once the dopamine in the seeking system kicks in, work can start to feel like a meaningful use of our time on the planet. We'll see how an activated seeking system allows work to let us test what we are capable of on our short journey of life.

In the next chapter, we'll look at some ways that leaders have encouraged self-expression to activate employees' seeking systems and help them consider their potential.

PART II

SELF—EXPRESSION

ENCOURAGING PEOPLE TO BRING THEIR BEST SELVES TO WORK

When Adesh woke up in his Delhi flat after a restless sleep, his mind was consumed with his first day at work at Wipro, an Indian information technology company.

Even though this was his fourth job since he left university two years ago, he was anxious about joining a new company. Making first impressions on coworkers, meeting everyone for the first time, struggling to fit in, making sure he is as good as everyone else: it was stressful.

He was worried about his new role, too. As a call-center rep, he'd be talking with people around the world and trying to solve their problems with their printers or booking their flights. This was all new to him. Sure, he'd done some chat support, but he'd never assisted anyone live, halfway around the world, on the phone before.

Even though this was a great job, Adesh knew it was going to be a grind. Since he'd be assisting customers in the United States, he'd need to be available during their business hours. His shifts would begin at 9:00 p.m. and go through the night. He'd need to deal calmly and professionally with frustrated customers, who could be rude and disrespectful. He'd also have to adopt a Western accent and attitude. No wonder new reps tended to quit after just a few months.

After an hour-long shuttle ride through Delhi traffic, Adesh arrived at the sprawling landscaped campus, where he was shown into a room along with eighteen other new hires. Having been onboarded a few times over the last two years, Adesh knew the drill. Soon, the admin types would show up, and Adesh and his classmates would have to fill out paperwork and sit through an hourslong orientation about their job responsibilities.

After a few minutes, a man walked through the door and introduced himself as a senior Wipro leader. Adesh was surprised: the man wasn't from HR. Instead of talking about procedures and responsibilities, the senior leader spent fifteen minutes discussing why Wipro was an outstanding organization. "Working at Wipro gives you the opportunity to express yourself," he told the group. Unlike most new-hire trainers, he didn't seem to be reading from a script.

After sharing personal stories about his Wipro experience, the man asked all the new hires to take a few minutes and write an answer to a question: "What is unique about you that leads to your happiest times and best performance at work? Reflect on a specific time—perhaps on a job, perhaps at home—when you were acting the way you were 'born to act.'"

Taken aback, Adesh stared at the blank piece of paper. He knew Wipro was different, but he hadn't expected to delve into his personal life at orientation. But, after a few moments, he was able to focus on the task at hand, and he thought about helping his twelve-year-old nephew Anil with his math homework.

As Adesh remembered, Anil couldn't understand how to use the rules of geometry to figure out the degrees of an angle. Frustrated and angry, Anil furiously erased his work and crumpled the paper. With a little effort, Adesh was able to calm Anil down. Then he walked him through the rules. "Look, Anil, a flat line is always 180 degrees," he said. "Let's write that here. And if you know this angle is 50 of those degrees, then how much does the other need to be?"

Adesh continued helping Anil in this fashion for thirty minutes, slowly and calmly helping him. It worked. Before long, Anil was really getting it, racing ahead without even asking questions, gathering confidence. When Adesh was leaving, Anil whispered, "Thank you for helping me." But Adesh didn't need to be told. He already saw the gratitude on Anil's face.

Now, at his job orientation, Adesh happily wrote down this memory.

"You haven't met each other yet," the Wipro staffer said after everyone was done writing, "but you'll be doing a lot of training together. So get together and introduce yourselves. But I want each of you to introduce your *best* self. Perhaps read the story you wrote and tell the group what it says about you at your best."

When it was his turn, Adesh told the group about helping Anil: "I'm good at empathizing with my nephew, seeing the block in his thinking. I like helping him get around that block."

After everybody finished, the leader gave each person a badge and a fleece sweatshirt customized with his or her name. Adesh felt good telling his story and listening to everyone else's. He felt that his new colleagues already knew a lot about him, and vice versa.

In this moment, he felt like his best self.

The Power of Best Impressions

We've all been in Adesh's shoes. When we join a new organization, the first few weeks are a blur: the confusing acronyms people throw at us, what topics are acceptable and unacceptable to discuss in meetings and over lunch, whether or not you should prioritize quality or speed. It's like visiting a foreign country—everything's unfamiliar, and we can't rely on our previous relationships, routines, and assumptions.

With all this ambiguity going on, this also is the time we experience the basic human need to fit in and be accepted by our new managers and coworkers.[1] It is a time of anxiety because it's a vulnerable situation to be in. Organizations know this, of course, which is why they traditionally have used this initial period to get us to absorb their values, their way of doing things.[2] Since new employees are a rapt, needy audience, it's easier for organizations to indoctrinate us to their norms, values, and expectations.

There's nothing wrong with this, per se. It's important for workers in organizations, especially big ones, to share a common purpose. But when my colleagues and I studied 605 new Wipro employees across three different operations centers in India, we discovered that there was a better way of conducting onboarding sessions.[3] As we confirmed in subsequent studies, an *individualized* approach to onboarding, where newcomers like Adesh write about and share stories about their best selves with others, leads to greater performance and retention. And perhaps more importantly, it connects employees more closely to their organizations.

In our experiment, we randomly assigned groups of new hires to one of three conditions. In the first condition, described above, employees were asked to write about times they used their best characteristics and then share them with the group. At the end of the session, participants were given a personalized badge and fleece sweatshirt.

In the second condition, after listening to a senior leader and a star performer talk about Wipro's values, and why Wipro is an outstanding organization, a different group of newcomers was asked to spend fifteen minutes reflecting on what they had just heard (e.g., "What did you hear about Wipro that makes you proud to be part of the organization?"). After discussing their answers with the group, people in this condition received a generic Wipro badge and fleece sweatshirt.

The participants in the third condition, the control group, went through Wipro's regular onboarding, which focused on skills training.

After tracking the participants for six months, we found that Adesh and his colleagues who were placed in the "best self" condition were outperforming their peers who had participated in Wipro's typical onboarding sessions. Their customers, for example, reported 11 percent higher satisfaction—72 percent compared with 61 percent. And, we found that the "best selves" cohort were more likely to remain in their jobs—retention improved by a whopping 32 percent! Compared with the control condition, results also showed that it helped to talk about Wipro's values (the second condition)—this reduced quitting by 14 percent but did not lead to significantly better customer satisfaction.

So in the end, asking people about their best selves and letting them share their ideas with their new peers worked the best—but in all my years of working with companies, I have not seen a company use this approach to onboarding.

Our Best Selves

At Wipro, we tried to perform what psychologists call a *wise intervention*.[4] A wise intervention is when you do something new and small that has disproportionately large effects because it fixes something that's making people feel emotionally vulnerable. Our experiment likely had a disproportionately large effect on Adesh and his fellow new hires because they were anxious about meeting new people and fitting in. In such situations, we tend to highlight the parts of ourselves that conform to the group and fit the expectations of others. This can be both exhausting and stressful.

The "best selves" intervention, however, alleviated this problem. By sharing their personal stories at the very start of their relationship, the new hires at Wipro were able to express themselves more fully by showing their colleagues their most valued behaviors and traits. As a consequence, they were viewed by their coworkers in the way they wanted to be seen. To put it another way, they felt like their best selves.

Does everybody have a best self? Remember, a self is just a story that we tell ourselves. It is not objective—you can't see it or touch it. But it is very real in the sense that the story affects how we act and how others respond to us. If we change the story we tell about ourselves, we change our behaviors.

As Laura Roberts and her colleagues at the University of Michigan have defined it, a best self is "the cognitive representation of the qualities and characteristics the individual displays when at his or her best."[5] Our concepts of our best selves are not projections of what we think we *could* become someday. Rather, they're based on our real-life experiences and actions. They comprise the skills and traits that we've developed and discovered over time, and the actions we have taken to affect others in a positive way.

The more our colleagues know who we are when we're at our best, the more likely we can feel like ourselves at work. We suspected that this is the reason why the people who experienced our wise intervention stayed so much longer and made clients happier: because they could express themselves more authentically. That would bond them to Wipro in a different way. As Amit Rastogi, one of the onboarding managers who helped with the study, told me: "People were proud to be recognized as individuals. This gave them a distinctive identity within the organization and helped them identify with the organizations much faster. They felt very connected to the organization at that time."

It's important to keep in mind that a best self is just one of a host of other identities that each of us inhabit depending on the circumstances. Sometimes our prominent identity might be as a father or a daughter, other times our identity as an academic, or manager, or writer might be prominent. The best self, like our other identities, needs to be activated. But as we saw at Wipro, it doesn't take much to do that. Because of our intervention, the new hires felt as if they were being encouraged to seek what was best and unique about themselves, and share this with colleagues as they were first meeting them, which gave additional meaning to their work.[6] This likely led them to exhibit their best character traits more often. And, since their coworkers and managers appreciated their unique skills and traits, they acted more freely and authentically in subsequent interactions.

The best thing about best-self activation is it creates long-term cascading effects. For example, after his best-self activation, Adesh experienced positive emotions such as enthusiasm, which in turn prompted more creative information processing.[7] And this resulted in more productive responses to stress.[8] Better creativity and more productive interactions with colleagues and customers further affirmed his best self, which lead to yet more positive emotions and performance, further affirming the self, and so on.

I've seen similar results in other studies, as well. For example, we recruited people to come into the lab and perform data entry tasks, and socialized them using the best-self approach. We found that, compared to a control condition, people in the best-self condition made fewer errors inputting the data, and they also were significantly more likely to come back and code more data on another day.[9] Their passion wasn't dampened after the session: once ignited, it continued to burn.

Why is this? As Janine Dutcher, a psychology professor at University of California, Los Angeles, has found via fMRI studies, when people are prompted to think about their best traits, their seeking systems are activated.[10] Dutcher and her team found no effects in control samples who made preference judgments that were not connected to their selves (they made judgments about toasters. Not that there's anything wrong with toasters). It turns us on to think about what we are capable of, and this is how our seeking systems help us bring more energy and engage more of ourselves at work.

You Are Bigger Than Your Job

As powerful as self-affirmation and self-expression are in improving our stories about ourselves and changing our behaviors, there's a way to increase their effects. Following the lead of the pioneering ideas published by Laura Roberts and her colleagues, we solicited best-self stories from people's social networks. That is, we asked an individual's friends, family, mentors, and coworkers to write narratives about times that individual made a distinct contribution.[11] For example, one person's friend wrote:

> You are unafraid to be intelligent. So many people, particularly women, are afraid to be the smartest person in the room. You are a wonderful role model for all bright, quick, and articulate women in the world, showing that it is more than ok to be clever and to allow people to see that you are smart. I can think of a time when you won the argument with the class, and I found it inspirational.

And here is an example narrative from a coworker:

> Laura has good forethought for business and does anything and everything she can to help keep us employed. In 2012, when Hurricane Sandy hit the East Coast, here in Florida we did not really think much of it. But Laura was obviously worried that it would impact her business, because a lot of our accounts receivables are in the NYC/New Jersey areas. She ended up borrowing from her retirement savings to keep the business going. I even suggested that maybe she could let the couple of part-timers go, but she responded that the people there always gave their best, so she wouldn't want to do anything less for them. It took about six months to get things back on track, but we all managed to keep our jobs thanks to Laura.

These stories from friends and colleagues were powerful for a couple reasons. First, they expanded people's views of themselves. Just as a fish doesn't know that it's wet, we don't always know our strengths because they seem so natural and normal to us. Our signature strengths don't seem like a big deal to us, but they mean so much to other people. As Peter Drucker wrote, "Most people think they know what they are good at. They are usually wrong. More often, people know what they are not good at—and even then more people are wrong than right."[12] And since the storytellers were trusted sources, their words were even more meaningful and impactful than self-reflection.

The benefits of these relational best-self activations from people's social networks are substantial. When our seeking systems are activated, our performance increases just as it did for the karaoke singers who interpreted their stress as excitement instead of anxiety. In a series of studies, Julia Lee, a professor at the University of Michigan, found that those who undergo relational best-self activation experience stronger immune responses, enhanced creative problem solving (over 200 percent improvement), and significantly less anxiety and negative physiological arousal. In another study, Lee randomly assigned half of the participants to read best-self stories from friends before giving a three-minute speech. These individuals were scored significantly more positively by a pair of independent judges than participants who wrote their own narratives.[13]

Self-Expression in Teams

Taken together, these studies present strong evidence that best-self activation is a trigger of the seeking system, resulting in better physical and mental functioning, and driving higher performance.

And the results suggest that it is more powerful to learn about your best self from others, compared to just thinking about it yourself.

Next, we wanted to examine whether relational best-self activation also can improve how teams function and perform. Effective communication and information sharing is needed for teams to reach peak performance. Unfortunately, when new teams are forming or when existing teams take on new members, newcomers can feel anxious about being accepted by the group. This anxiety can make new members withhold unique information that might make them stand out.[14] It's safer, after all, to just discuss information that everyone agrees on if we want others in the team to see us as competent.[15] We wondered if we could help new teams avoid this trap by using their social networks to activate their seeking systems.

We focused on team performance in a sample of 246 senior leaders who participated in a four-week leadership development program at Harvard's Kennedy School. There were a total of forty-two teams, which we randomly split into two experimental conditions. All participants completed a self-reflection, where they wrote their own stories about their best impact on others. In one condition, senior leaders received the relational self-affirmation reports, produced by Essentic, before participating in a crisis simulation related to public health.[16] The teams in the control group condition didn't receive their reports until the study concluded.

Each diverse team played the role of an emergency watch squad in a seven-day simulation. Following the report of a dangerous coronavirus detected in their state, the teams had to work as part of the state government to monitor developments and propose a solution.

Participants in both conditions received identical information (drip-fed from tweets, news stories, etc.) leading up to the briefing day. They had to react to and make decisions about the information, and then propose a way forward. The team members had never met or communicated with each other before the simulation began, so our relational best-self affirmation was the only difference between treatment and control teams. On the day of the briefing, each team made a twenty-minute presentation to a panel of experts consisting of individuals from the US government and Harvard faculty members. The expert panels (a total of sixteen judges) assessed the quality and creativity of the solutions, and did not know that different teams received different treatments. So we had a good measure of the teams' performance. The results revealed that the teams assigned to the best-self expression condition outperformed those in the control condition, even after controlling for cohort, team size, mean age, and gender composition.

In his book *Crossing the Unknown Sea,* David Whyte says: "Companies need the contributing vitality of all the individuals who work for them in order to stay alive in the sea of changeability in which they find themselves. They must find a real way of asking people to bring these hidden heartfelt qualities to the workplace. A way that doesn't make them feel manipulated or the subject of some 5 year plan."[17]

It's up to leaders in organizations to address this problem, and activating people's best selves and triggering their seeking systems is a great way to do it for two reasons.

First, this is good for us as human beings because we are more likely to feel alive at work. Research shows that when people identify and use their unique strengths, they report feeling "more alive" or "intensely alive."[18] In one study, psychologist Martin Seligman randomly assigned one set of participants to learn about their "signature strengths" by taking an inventory of character strengths (you can take it too: www.authentichappiness.org), and were asked to use one of these top strengths in a new way every day for one week. Compared with a control group, people in the signature strengths condition had fewer depressive symptoms (including headaches, trouble sleeping, and trouble waking up).[19] That's because when people seek, find, and fulfill what is best and unique about themselves, it gives meaning and direction to their lives.[20]

Second, if we feel like work is more like "real life," complete with intrinsic motivation and positive emotions, we're more apt to help our organizations adapt, innovate, and stay relevant. This can pay huge dividends to organizations, including, as David Whyte writes, "more adaptability, vitality, imagination, and the enthusiastic willingness to go the extra mile—qualities which are ancient and which humans have wanted for themselves since the beginning of recorded history."[21]

This is the new war for talent—not wooing employees away from competitors, but unleashing the enthusiasm that is already there within employees, but dormant.

In chapter 4, we look at ways other organizations have experimented with employee self-expression.

CHAPTER 4

PROMOTING SELF—EXPRESSION

When Adam Grant, a best-selling author and professor at Wharton, was a PhD student, he and fellow student Justin Berg volunteered at the Make-a-Wish Foundation. This nonprofit's mission is to "grant the wishes of children with life-threatening medical conditions and enrich the human experience with hope, strength, and joy."

With this noble mission, Make-a-Wish is able to recruit top talent. But as Grant and Berg's volunteering turned into a qualitative investigation, they interviewed employees and discovered that the work can be grueling. As employees help the Make-a-Wish kids, they must deal with a lot of loss, sadness, and grief, which can lead to emotional exhaustion and burnout. One staff member said: "You don't want to think about it all the time, because it's really,

really sad. That's the part that's most emotionally draining—thinking about what these kids are going through, realizing that they're in and out of the doctor every day, and the strain that it puts on the parents."[1]

During the course of their interviews, Grant and Berg observed an interesting policy that then-CEO Susan Fenters Lerch implemented in order to help curb burnout. While at a development conference at Disneyland, she learned that employees are encouraged to invent their own job titles to describe their unique values, identities, and talents. Intrigued, Lerch floated the idea to other senior leaders at the foundation, and they decided to encourage self-reflective titles at Make-a-Wish.

Lerch's goal was simple. She hoped that self-reflective titles would help employees remember that even though their work was emotionally difficult, their ultimate mission was to bring joy.[2] She invited all employees to create their own titles to supplement their formal titles, and emphasized that employees could reflect their most important roles and identities in the organization.

For her part, Lerch deliberately selected a lighthearted title—"Fairy Godmother of Wishes"—that would make people smile and remember the good outcomes of their work. Examples of other titles included "Minister of Dollars and Sense" (COO), "Goddess of Greetings" (administrative assistant), "Magic Messenger" and "Heralder of Happy News" (PR managers), "Duchess of Data" (database manager), and "Merry Memory Maker" (wish managers).

Employees received business cards that featured their new titles alongside their formal titles. The titles also were added to the chapter's website, and employees expanded their email signatures to include them.

What's in a Name?

Could such a minor change, which didn't cost any money, actually affect employees' attitudes and behaviors?

Grant and Berg were both a little skeptical about the titles, but in their interviews, employees raved about their titles without prompting. These interviews revealed that 85 percent of the employees said that the self-reflective titles helped reduce their exhaustion. One employee, for example, said that his self-created title "just makes [work] easier and cushions the blow a little bit and keeps things inspiring." A training manager said that her title "helps you realize that, although this is a severe situation, you can still focus on the joy that is left."

Intrigued by what Grant and Berg had uncovered, we decided to dig deeper into the recordings of employees' interview responses, and we uncovered three common themes. First, 69 percent of the interviewees said that self-reflective titles let them bring their personal identity into the organization. As we learned in chapter 3, self-affirmation and self-expression activate people's seeking systems, which increases enthusiasm, decreases burnout, and makes them more open and creative. For example, the manager of operations, who—like Grant and Berg—was initially skeptical of the titles, described how her title gives her work personal meaning and lets others to appreciate her role:

> I would describe myself as the "accountant type," where, if something sounds or seems silly to me, then I wouldn't be comfortable with that. But being considered "Keeper of Keys and Grounds" doesn't sound silly to me. It gives a pretty good visual of what I do. [The titles] allow staff to get to know each other better. If we didn't have [them], I think we would have higher staff turnover . . . people would get burned out.

A wish manager said:

> When I tell people [my title], they say, "That's so you—it fits you so well." You fit right in there . . . It makes you want to come into work . . . If [the titles] didn't happen, we wouldn't know each other as well. I don't think it would be as personal for some people.

A second theme in employees' comments was psychological safety: employees described how the titles opened people up and helped change the culture inside the organization to encourage information sharing and unique ideas. Amy Edmondson, a professor at Harvard Business School, defined psychological safety as the degree to which employees feel comfortable taking interpersonal risks.[3] For many employees (77 percent), the titles opened the door for colleagues to view one another as human beings, not merely job holders. For example, one employee remarked:

> Having permission to take up fun titles . . . It helps to feel more at ease with other coworkers [by] allowing some barriers to be broken . . . that environment encourages people to lay their difficulties on the table and try to work things out together.

Likewise, a volunteer services manager said:

> At first, it took a little while to get used to, coming from a much more business-oriented nonprofit. After I got used to the title, I really appreciated it . . . [it] reminds you that the environment is not so strict . . . The titles have a way of affecting everyone's thought process—people are much more open to ideas . . . It keeps the stress level lower than what it could be—makes it much easier to interact with one another and connect.

Here is what CEO Lerch said:

> Every single solitary person on the planet has a story, and [the titles] help you keep that in perspective . . . It humanizes everyone . . . It breaks down barriers and allows a genuine conversation . . . What we're doing is so intense . . . you have to create a fun and supportive place for people to feel comfortable so that when they're faced with a tragic situation, they can deal with it.

71

Finally, many employees described how their self-reflective titles helped express their personal identity to people *outside* Make-
a-Wish. In particular, lots of participants (85 percent) mentioned
the self-reflective titles helped them create enjoyable interactions
with outsiders. For example, the CFO explained how the job title
serves as "an icebreaker for people we meet; it opens up dialogue."
A wish manager said:

> There's nothing better to meet someone new and say, "I'm
> a wish manager, also known as a 'fairy tale pixie.'" It opens
> up conversation: "Oh, what does a fairy tale pixie do?" . . .
> It gives you a little pick-me-up when you hear that; it's fun,
> unexpected, and enjoyable.

A development team leader explained:

> Most people love to hear these titles. It's fun, different, and
> magic to these people—they want to be a part of it. It em-
> powers people to have fun and to translate that fun to the
> community . . . it just makes [work] easier and cushions the
> blow a little bit and keeps things inspiring.

Through subsequent studies, Grant, Berg, and I saw self-
affirmative titles work in other organizations and industries. At
Novant Health, a health-care system in the southeastern United
States, the trend in the data was strong and clear: employees
who brainstormed new titles—say, "Germ Slayer" (physician who
deals with infectious diseases), "Quick Shot" (nurse who gives

allergy shots to children), or "Bone Seeker" (x-ray technician)—experienced an 11 percent decrease in burnout across time, while employees in the control groups did not.

It warms the heart to see the seeking system at work this way. Self-reflective titles aren't just fun names. Because they encourage self-reflection and self-expression, personalized titles trigger positive emotions and a greater sense of purpose. Most of all, they encourage us to "cognitively reappraise" our work.[4] In other words, they nudge us to focus on the more meaningful and intrinsically rewarding elements of our jobs, which we're prone to lose sight of.

Self-Expression in Teams

Self-reflective titles don't only affect the individuals that adopt them; they also can improve team dynamics.

Lindy Greer and her colleagues at Stanford Business School recruited eighty startup teams from Silicon Valley and Silicon Beach incubators, and gave each team eighteen minutes to build the highest tower possible using spaghetti, paper, and tape.[5] The structure also had to be able to support a marshmallow. If you think it sounds easy, try it. It takes a lot of creativity, experimentation, and collaboration to pull it off—and can lead to a lot of frustration as the competition unfolds.

With some teams, Greer and her colleagues asked each participant to create job titles that "best suits your talents, strengths, and passions . . . and clearly expresses your unique contribution to the team." In addition, they asked the entrepreneurs to write job descriptions that included "what responsibilities and tasks would fall within such a role." From there, participants were asked to share their titles and descriptions with their team members.

The individuals in this condition put their minds to it and created titles that reflected the unique value they thought they brought to the teams: "Second Violin," "Defender of the Codebase," "Godfather of Product Design," "Chief Schmoozing Officer," "Chief Banana Wrangler," "Chief Social Butterfly," "The Scottie Pippen of Development," "Taylor Swift of Sales," and "Sultan of Strategy."

As I'm sure you've guessed, the researchers found huge differences between the teams with self-reflective titles and those without. Why?

First, collaborating on the tower required an activated seeking system to promote curiosity, experimenting, play, and sharing creative ideas. But another reason emerged in the entrepreneurial setting: since startups start small and scale quickly, they often lack the clear-cut hierarchies that exist in more established organizations. As a result, team members aren't always sure who's taking the lead during different stages of collaborative projects, which can lead to indecisiveness. By adopting their own titles and sharing them, however, everyone in the group had a clearer understanding of the others' roles, which led to more decisiveness. There was less ambiguity. Everyone knew who was best at what and what people took pride in, and they delegated accordingly.

Together, these studies suggest that unique, self-reflective titles allow employees to realize the "*me* in the *we*."[6] This allows employees to have a distinct personal identity within a team. As psychologist Marilyn Brewer would say, it allows each team member to be "optimally distinctive."[7]

Interventions that stimulate people's seeking systems through self-expression can have big effects, because team members bring more of themselves to teams when they are less fearful and more playful.[8] Robin Ely and David Thomas, two professors at Harvard University, saw this in action when they studied a consulting firm, a financial services firm, and a law firm. The researchers discovered that when teams openly discussed the unique qualities of each team member, and then tried to integrate their diverse perspectives into the group's decision making, employees felt more valued and respected and were more willing to offer their take on things. In turn, this enhanced the team's learning and performance. And it transformed their team's diversity into an asset, as it should be, rather than a hindrance to communication.[9]

The last point, about diversity, is important. Good leaders know that they need to build teams comprising people with different backgrounds, skills, and perspectives. But as we saw in the last chapter with the teams at the Harvard Kennedy School, if team members aren't willing to express themselves and their viewpoints, the teams won't reap the benefits of diversity. In fact, William Swann, a professor of Psychology at the University of Texas. worked with Jeffrey Polzer at Harvard, and found that diverse teams performed *worse* than homogenous teams when members felt as if their unique strengths were not being recognized.[10]

Over the years, organizations have spent lots of energy and money trying to improve team creativity and decision making: diversity training, self-managed teams, and cross-functional teams. These improvements can work, but a far simpler, more human-oriented approach can work wonders while costing much less. We need to think beyond the mechanistic, de-individuated way we treated employees during the Industrial Revolution, and start lighting up people's seeking systems with self-expression at work.

The Organization as a Self-Expression Vehicle

Brandon Rigoni and Jim Asplund from the Gallup Institute described a huge dataset from millions of employees across the world. The results from this data showed that the more hours per day adults believe they use their unique strengths, the more likely they are to report "being energetic," "learning something interesting," "being happy," and "smiling or laughing a lot."[11] These are the outcomes that the seeking system produces.

In fact, employees who use their strengths every day also are more than *three times* more likely to report having an excellent quality of life. That's what I mean by activating a life more worth living. Although these Gallup Institute findings are correlational, they complement the seeking system evidence and the results from the field experiments and they show the seeking system at work across national borders and company cultures.

The self-affirmation and self-expression processes described in this chapter and chapter 3—such as the Wipro onboarding process, and the relational best-self reports we gave to the leaders in the Harvard program—represent *strengths-based management techniques.* The Gallup data described above also looked at the business unit outcomes of companies that have put into practice strengths-based developmental coaching and job crafting that allows employees to do more of what they do best. These are practices that affirm employees' unique strengths and encourage them to use their strengths more often. The study included 49,495 business units with 1.2 million employees across twenty-two organizations in seven industries and forty-five countries.

Results suggested that work groups receiving a strengths intervention realized the same types of improvements that I reported at Novant Health Wipro and the teams at Harvard: 3–7 percent increases in customer engagement, 9–15 percent increases in engaged employees, and 26–72 percent decreases in employee quitting. Rigoni and Asplund also reported some impressive outcomes that I had not yet seen, including 10–19 percent greater sales, 14–29 percent greater profit, and 22–59 percent fewer safety incidents.

If we look at our widespread social addiction to Instagram, Facebook, and Music.ly—not to mention *World of Warcraft*—we start to see how sticky and interesting activities become when they start with self-expression. Philosophers have been telling us for millennia that people have an innate drive to show others who they really are. As humans, we want to feel affirmed for our authentic selves.[12]

As logical and as evidence-based as this may seem, most organizations are failing us in this regard. Organizational life often runs afoul of the human desire for self-expression. Remember, the original goal of management was to *depersonalize* work, so that employees could be substituted quickly into roles and evaluated in a standardized, impersonal way.[13]

But even as the demands on employees have shifted toward creativity and innovation, we still see bureaucratic job titles, inflexible roles, and systems that generate fear and deperson-alization instead of excitement, self-expression, and creativity. Think about forced-ranking performance evaluation systems that *insist* on leaders identifying at least half of their employees as below average. Depersonalized approaches to management will fail even more with newer generations, who place even more emphasis on self-expression and meaningful work than previous generations.[14]

This is why I believe there is a big win out there for firms that think of themselves as platforms for employees' self-expression. If organizations get this right, work becomes an outlet that employ-ees want. Self-expression organizations activate employees' seek-ing systems, resulting in enthusiasm and the intrinsic motivation to invest their best back into the companies (see figure 4-1). Of course, it is not realistic to think that employment at one firm will last forever: employees need to look at their careers "as a series of tours of duty . . . less like ladders and more like jungle gyms."[15] But it *is* realistic that leaders can help employees learn about, ex-press, and practice playing to their unique strengths. This means that employees get more living out of life in the short term (remem-ber, dopamine = free, legal drugs) while improving their "portable selves"—that is, increasing their value and contributions in future roles with future employers. Who is losing here?

FIGURE 4-1

Self-expression activates the seeking system

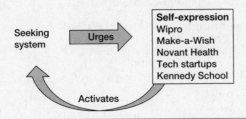

And it doesn't take much to make this happen, not much money anyway. What it takes is a new mindset. Leaders can still maintain the frame while they build more productive and meaningful relationships with employees by helping them articulate, project, and use their best selves at work. In fact, leaders *need* to ensure the continuity and focus of the organization. We need agility, not fragility, in organizations. So we need to find a middle ground.

The examples we've explored in this chapter and in chapter 3 are illustrations of that middle ground. As we saw, a little bit of strategic focus on self-affirmation and self-expression can ignite employees' seeking systems and generate enthusiasm and creativity that helps organizations thrive.

Employers should create best-self reports for employees and for new teams, and then encourage employees to re-craft their jobs so they can play to their strengths. Employers can legitimize self-expressive job titles from the top down, as employees customize their jobs and their job titles from the bottom up. Leaders can encourage teams to openly discuss the unique qualities of each team member, and include members' perspectives into the group's decision making. These are evidence-based ways that employees can engage meaningful parts of their self-concepts within the standards of their business environment.

What is holding us back?

PART III

EXPERIMENTATION

CHAPTER 5

ENCOURAGING SERIOUS PLAY

After twelve years, you'd think Luigi would be used to waking up at 4:30 a.m., but the sound of his alarm clock is like a punch to his stomach. Lured by the smell of coffee wafting from his timer-controlled espresso machine, he drags himself out of bed. In the kitchen, he downs a shot and forces himself to eat a croissant before leaving.

The plant has been stressful lately. A few months ago, Alessandro, the general manager, told Luigi and his fellow workers that corporate was threatening to shut down the facility if they didn't reduce the number of defects in the cooktops and washing machines they made. The defects were costly. Even when someone caught them before the items shipped, they had to be fixed, which took time. Defects were even more costly when the products "escaped" the plant: customers were unhappy and then initiated expensive warranty processes.

So Luigi was anxious after the ultimatum from corporate. Since he didn't want to be the one who made the error that closed the plant, he'd been trying to focus a lot more on each of his board solders, making sure the connections were strong. But he couldn't help comparing himself with others. His part of the process sometimes took almost two minutes to do correctly, and he had trouble keeping up, especially with his friend Thomas, who stood next to him on the line, whose task took just under two minutes. As the pile between him and Thomas stacked up, he could feel his heart beating like a drum.

Unfortunately, the increased efforts of Luigi and his coworkers weren't enough. A few months after corporate's ultimatum to reduce defects, Alessandro huddled everyone together in the main area. Luigi knew it was bad news. He could tell by the look in Alessandro's eyes. As the general manager began to speak, Luigi braced himself. Alessandro gave the crew the news: they were going to shut down operations in Luigi's line, but the employees were going to be trained while the line was closed. Alessandro said the factory was introducing lean manufacturing, which meant that the workers were going to have to learn an entirely new process.

While it was better than losing their jobs, this was still bad news for many of the employees. For their entire careers, they had specialized in a small part of a larger process: for example, one person attached the serpentine to the chassis. Another person connected and installed the electronic panel, and so on. Individual workers had to worry only about their part of the process. This was all going to change, and they were unhappy, skeptical, and apprehensive.

Now, on this the first day of training, Luigi doesn't know what to expect. This won't be on-the-job training, as the line is shut down. And, Alessandro has brought in two internal change management specialists, Robin and Hadrian, to help them learn the new approach. To start, Robin and Hadrian teach the workers about a single lean concept called "pull-not-push" manufacturing. Rather than making as many high-quality parts as possible and passing them on, each person gives the next worker a part only when that worker asks for it—the exact *opposite* of what Luigi had been taught to do and had perfected over the last eight years on the job.

To demonstrate, Robin and Hadrian use Legos to assemble little cars, then ask the workers to participate. Luigi is doubtful at first. Legos? It beats working, sure, but aren't Legos for kids?

The team begins building the Lego car according to their old approach to manufacturing. One person puts the wheels on the hubs and attaches them to the chassis, then hands the part on. The next person builds the fenders above each wheel, another puts the doors on. And each person makes as many of his assemblies as possible and passes them along to the next person.

Soon enough, the group runs into familiar problems. Since some people are taking longer than others, the parts start stacking up, and half-built cars start rolling off the table and breaking, so they have to be remade.

Then Robin asks the teams to design a new layout for the car production process, using the "pull-not-push" approach. He says, "Don't give the next person your part until they ask for it." This forces the team to think about the flow of the new process and the signals governing it. Once each team has designed a few potential solutions, Robin invites them to present the ideas and discuss them as a group. They converge on one of the ideas, which they then actually put into place for making the little cars. They practice for an hour, trying out the new assembly process and getting familiar with how it feels to work this way.

For Luigi, the hour flies by. Although he's still somewhat skeptical about the new process, he appreciates that the instructors weren't just divulging information. They asked the workers for their input, and they listened.

This learning-playing sequence occurs four times over two days. In each session, Robin and Hadrian teach the team a new concept of lean; then the team redesigns the car process using the new concept; then they implement one of their solutions in their Lego factory; and finally they practice the new process so that they internalize it and make it their own.

After two days of work on the car-building process, the changes are astounding: more product, fewer defects, less stress, lower inventory. People actually are enthusiastic, which many of them have not felt at work for a long time. Despite the dark cloud hanging over the factory, the workers laugh and joke with each other, and they are curious to see how the new process would work.

They feel playful—and energized.

Creating Safe Zones

According to affective neuroscientists Jason Wright and Jaak Panksepp, one way to activate people's seeking systems is to create an experimental "safe zone" that includes play and supportive social bonding. Play is important because it recruits, or stimulates, the seeking system, which in turn attenuates activity in the negative emotion systems.[1] Panksepp and his coauthors write, "Play can promote emotional resilience, diminish the negative affective consequences of stressful emotional experiences, and fertilize affectively positive gene expression patterns."[2]

Although Wright and Panksepp were writing about clients in psychotherapy sessions, their advice is applicable to workers as well: to get people to change their mindsets and their behaviors, you need to diminish their negative emotions and let them experiment with something new in order to learn some new behaviors. In other words, you need to encourage some freedom in the frame.

It sounds a bit counterintuitive to many people that play and experimentation are most important when things seem negative and threatening. But as was explained to me by Robin, we can see this in action with Luigi and his fellow factory workers. Like the new hires at Wipro, they were in a vulnerable position. Already stressed by the threat of the plant closing, they had to learn a completely new process that overturned everything they knew and practiced throughout their careers. So it's no surprise they were on edge.

An anxious workforce isn't good for anyone involved, especially when learning is needed. When fear is in the air, it's like the cat fur experiment described in chapter 2: workers are less playful and less receptive to new information. Obviously, their instructors would be less effective in this situation. This was evident when corporate tried its "burning platform" approach to reducing defects. Sure, the employees had worked with more urgency, since they knew their jobs were at stake. But the outcomes speak for themselves: the number of defects wasn't reduced because the defects were from a *process* problem, not a motivation problem. Everyone kept doing the same things they were doing with more focus, but the faulty process was not changed.

But by making a deep investment in a risk-free zone for learning, practicing, and playing, the factory activated employees' seeking systems. The instructors made sure that mistakes didn't matter (workers practiced with Lego cars, not cooktops that needed to ship). They allowed the group to learn and experiment without negative consequences. Because of this, the group's seeking systems ramped up and their fear was tamped down.

Experimental safe zones also created *intrinsic motivations*, which are much more powerful than extrinsic motivations because they unleash creativity. Instead of working hard for fear of losing their jobs (extrinsic), Luigi and his colleagues were fueled by their own enthusiasm and curiosity (intrinsic). This in turn transformed their attitudes about the change.[3] Instead of being skeptical—as they were at the beginning—by the end, they were itching to explore and take the experiments farther.

Curiosity is a potent emotion. And when everyone on a team is curious, they are more likely to move away from their comfort zones and old habits, and work together in new ways.

Paying Lip Service to Creativity

Remember our unconscious bias against creativity and innovation (chapter 3)? We all like to think that we're open to new ideas, but in reality, we're often resistant to change and new ideas, even those of us with loads of education. For example, Harvard's Amy Edmondson studied why some medical teams did not adopt a new method of open-heart surgery, even though it was safer, less invasive and painful, and improved recovery time. As it turns out, the newness of the procedure, which involved special equipment to access the heart through an incision between the ribs, was a source of anxiety. For doctors who had mastered their craft—and a delicate and difficult one at that—the new procedure presented the chance of failure. They were afraid to learn because they had to give up control and depend more on their nursing team. Even though the new approach was better for patients, many doctors continued with the old approach, and lost relevance.

The lesson here, according to Edmondson, is:

> When work is not framed as an opportunity to "get it right" on the first try, workers may be more able to learn in the process and ultimately to get it right than when work is framed as an opportunity to perform, to shine, or to execute perfectly. The process of trial and reflection is most successful when participants are open to change . . . that is, they may have observed or interpreted something in a different way or may have different information at the outset.

89

To even consider this possibility, however, requires either an innate or trained habit of being curious.[4]

Edmondson's study corroborates the more general literature showing that framing change as a chance to experiment and learn is important for activating the emotions of the seeking systems. When people frame a task as a performance situation, it triggers anxiety and they become more risk averse and less willing to persist than people who frame the same task as a learning situation and trigger curiosity.[5] Frame a task as a performance situation, and people actually learn less because they engage in less experimentation. And they are less likely to formulate new strategies in difficult situations, and instead fall back on the ineffective strategies they have used in the past. This is why the medical teams needed to practice communication and collaboration together before moving to real patients. And why Luigi and his team played with Legos and learned new behaviors outside the context of normal cooktop production.

From Play to Production

Anyone who has read about lean manufacturing knows that the initiative will fail if employees feel that the executive team does not support them or respect their efforts.[6] Discouragement takes hold and the lean effort takes a nosedive. But many managers don't know how to convert their support and respect for manufacturing teams into the types of exploration and learning activities described above. They are not clear how to ignite employees' seeking systems and generate the necessary emotions to experiment, invent, and bring enthusiasm to the change. And if employees do start to get excited and make plans for changes but then are not given the chance to move their plans forward, they become disillusioned and their support of lean manufacturing activities dies.[7]

In other words, once people's seeking systems are activated, especially in a learning environment, it's important for leaders to ride that wave and unleash their potential. This is what the trainers at the factory did. The dopamine flooding the workers' brains was not only making them feel good but also opening them to learning.[8] The workers were curious to push what they had learned farther—a little like the way Bonnie Nardi and other gamers experience *World of Warcraft*.

At this point, the workers felt comfortable—and eager—to apply what they learned to white goods. They were ready to translate the lean manufacturing steps they had used to build the Lego cars—integrating pull-not-push and zero defects and load-balancing the work processes—to making their own products. Contrast this with many change initiatives, where the changes are designed by consultants and cascaded down to reluctant, wary, anxious employees.

At this point, the assembly team (plus Robin and Hadrian) met with Alessandro to present what they had been working on all week. As the team told Alessandro what effect the changes would have on the factory, he could see their enthusiasm. Alessandro heard, for the first time as manager, workers *asking* to improve their work routines. It was clear that the workers *wanted* to use their ideas. Based on their ideas and enthusiasm, Alessandro encouraged the team to try and redesign how their production line worked.

Because the workers were actively involved in the training, and because their seeking systems were activated, they were able to come up with lots of creative solutions and ideas. Working with Robin and Hadrian, they rethought their own work processes, redesigned their work spaces, and changed who was responsible for different steps. They also came up with a big idea: rather than workers stacking all their parts beside them to pull from all day, they could put all the parts needed for any given unit (e.g., a cooktop or a dryer) on a cart that followed the unit around.

At the end of the workweek, the team was still eager to continue their planning. In fact, most of the team came into work on Saturday to finalize the plans, which is unheard of at a unionized plant. In Italy.

On Monday the teams presented their plan to Alessandro. It was not perfect, but it was well on track. Alessandro was impressed, not only with the ideas, but with the zest he could see in the team as they presented, and with the ownership that came through their voices. He said, "Really good work. Let's do it. We'll hand the whole plan over to engineering and ask them to implement it as soon as possible." But Robin and Hadrian asked if the assembly-line workers could experiment with the implementation themselves.

This went directly against the cultural norms. Changing a work process at this facility would usually require the engineering department to get the right tools and equipment and processes in place. For example, just the "part cart" that would follow the unit around could take months. Engineering would take their time getting design specs, offers, and a contract with a supplier; then wait for the supplier to build it. This meant going back to the old way of production for at least two months, which didn't sound very good to the production team. After all this experimenting and learning, that sounded like working.

Robin agreed: "Let's just see what we can accomplish in two weeks. What is a cart? It's a platform with wheels. Let's skip the engineers and get some wheels and make some carts [they actually ended up using shopping trolleys from the local supermarket]. Let's find a way to clear some space for all the excess inventory." In this way, the production workers spent another week making their own vision into a working reality, leaving themselves time to test the actual changes.

Remember, this whole time, the team was not producing any appliances. Even though the other two lines were operating, the facility's leaders made a big investment in getting the employees excited, knowledgeable, and committed to lean manufacturing. As Robin told me:

> There are really only two important elements to making
> transformation work: giving people ownership of the vision
> of what it should look like, and giving them a safe space to
> try, experiment, and fail. This is why, after the team had
> the vision, we set this crazy time frame—two weeks—and
> just gave them space to mess around. Of course, it can't be
> perfect in two weeks. Nothing *needs* it to be perfect. We
> gave people lots of room for failure, by saying "Let's just get
> *something* done in two weeks." I said to the team, "I know it
> won't be perfect, but your plan is good. So let's experiment."
> Hadrian would ask, "Is anyone willing to try to put together

shelving today?" and two people would work on it for a half a day and we'd have customized shelving.

Robin also told me:

The fact that you're not contracting out expensive changes makes everyone feel more relaxed about the entire experiment. This makes it feel closer to the Lego simulation than it does to the factory's jobs they perform day in, day out.

In two weeks, Luigi and the rest of the production team made lean manufacturing their own. They applied it to their line and experimented with the process until it worked. The line was now completely rearranged and revised, and the employees were more energized than they had been in years, maybe for decades. It looked a bit Frankenstein, with plenty of temporary fixes and halfway solutions. But it was good enough to do the job, according to Robin and Hadrian, who told me that their job was to take the blame if it didn't work.

When I talk with leaders about creating employee enthusiasm and excitement, they often push back by talking about the boring industry in which they work, or the boring jobs that their employees have to do. In one session, a senior leader told us: "Oh, sure, it would be easy to develop an excited workforce if we worked at Apple or Amazon, but unfortunately we work in insurance claims. It's just not an industry where people get excited."

What gives me the most hope about the seeking system is that it doesn't care what industry you operate in. It doesn't care if you are making washing machines, or tires, or selling insurance. Employees may be in a state of learned helplessness, but their seeking systems are urging them to think about the cause and effect of their behaviors, and to experiment with new ways of solving problems and finding resources. The dopamine is on standby, ready to surge and push aside negative emotions.

What I find hopeful, and fascinating, is how the same work making the same product can become more engaging to employees when their seeking systems are activated, and they have a chance to be curious and try new things. The same workers who view their work as just a boring job can change their attitudes and behaviors when their seeking systems are triggered. An activated seeking system is not about what you are making, it's about how and why you are making it. Once the dopamine is flowing, employees gain more enthusiasm and commitment to their work.

For example, in Luigi's white-goods facility, after the employees started making products according to their new process, the union tried to block them. Here's what happened: first, four enraged union leaders stormed into Alessandro's office shouting "No way! This is not going to happen. First, you can't change the shifts. That is already in the contract. Second, you can't combine these two jobs, because those are negotiated as separate rates."

It was only the employees' enthusiasm and commitment to their work that allowed the progress to continue. When the union leader went to tell the production team the changes were off, the employees protested: "But this is *our* plan. Why are you blocking it?" The union leaders told the employees the whole plan was a trick to eliminate their jobs. The workers were puzzled and asked, "Who are you representing here? We want to do it." In the end, due to the workers' enthusiasm, the union leaders agreed that they could try the new approach for six months. This was the first time the workers negotiated with their own union.

In just three months, Luigi's line reduced internal defects by 30 percent, productivity was up 25 percent, and in-plant inventory was down over 90 percent. Defect rates and inventory in the other lines in the same facility didn't change.

In this chapter, we saw how serious play becomes when leaders need employees to learn new skills and help the organization survive. We saw how fear-based approaches to change, which threaten employees with burning platforms, get employees' attention but not their creativity, commitment, or learning. Using play and experimentation to activate employees' seeking systems is a necessary skill for leaders who need their organization to adapt and thrive in a changing environment.

In chapter 6, we'll look at several other approaches that leaders have used in different cultures to ignite employees' seeking systems and prompt new products, services, and approaches to work. We will also see how leaders need to "experiment with experimenting" in order to get the balance right, and why this is actually an important part of modeling a learning mindset.

CHAPTER 6

EXPANDING ON FREEDOM AND CREATIVITY

Lipot can't believe it's already 11:30. *At night.* He and his team have been programming nonstop for ten hours, only taking breaks to go to the bathroom. He has not worked with this particular combination of colleagues before. It's the most fun that he's had at work in years—perhaps ever—and he's surprised how excited they are to see how far they can push their idea. On a Thursday night, he'd usually be going out with his friends to the ruin bars of Budapest and enjoying their decayed opulence. But his team's iPhone app seems to be starting to work, and Lipot finds he wants to keep programming to get his piece of the prototype done.

Part of the thrill today is making this much progress this fast—from design to functional prototype in less than a day. And it is so satisfying for the three-person team to dive really deep into a project of their own design. Usually Lipot needs to break up his time between four or five different "headache problems," none of which is really a design issue, and all of which demand more time than he can dedicate before moving on to fight the next fire.

As a member of Dealogic's engineering team, which includes developers, architects, and testers, Lipot writes and tests the code that ultimately allows clients to do deals. This group, spread over the globe, deals with a lot of pressure. As you might guess, perfection is expected when hundreds of millions of dollars are at stake. So Lipot's job usually involves carrying out relatively mundane coding tasks: updates and improvements to software that is already highly functional, hitting targets and launch dates. Not creating new programming that solves new problems.

Initially, Lipot was a little suspicious when his manager first described this new one-day corporate initiative in an email. On top of everything else on his plate, now he was supposed to come up with a personal project he wanted to work on, then put together a team to work on it. He remembered thinking: "Really? How much can we really accomplish in twenty-four hours?" Much of which, realistically, was going to be dedicated to sleeping and eating.

But he felt things start to change when he began formulating his "back of the napkin" pet project. His idea was to use some AI to scan the internet and then auto-text someone when a given company started trending in the news. He talked to some other programmers with some of the needed skills and they got excited too, and suddenly he was looking forward to trying some of the ideas out. He'd never have gotten around to those ideas otherwise.

Now that they are deeply involved in the task, today feels very different from most days to Lipot and his impromptu team. It's satisfying to be enthusiastic and "locked in" to an activity—to be pulled along by the current of the work rather than forcing yourself to push through it.

Cracks in the Culture

As Dealogic matured from small startup to a major international player, Toby Haddon, its COO, started to see some cracks in the culture. Demand for Dealogic's services had grown briskly over the last twenty years. To keep quality high in the face of growth, managers kept refining internal processes, which included quantifiable performance metrics.

Ordinarily, process refinement sounds pretty good if you are a COO. But it can also present long-term problems, which I touched on in chapter 2: it can replace intrinsic motivation with extrinsic motivation. KPIs and the accompanying career implications lead the fear system to dominate the seeking system, taking creativity and enthusiasm down with it.[1] The extrinsic rewards crowd out the intrinsic buzz.

This was beginning to happen at Dealogic. Haddon saw less zest. Fewer employees were turned on by what they did every day. Employee enthusiasm was drifting downward as anxiety about performance metrics was on the rise. Programmers showed less enjoyment of elegant programming, and focused more on whether they would receive their bonuses. Instead of thinking about their work in terms of learning how to do cool new things and mastering new languages or approaches, employees talked about their work in terms of KPI targets.

Haddon watched as some of the best developers and architects in both Budapest and London started to get bored and switched off. Not just emotionally switched off, either: people were applying for more interesting jobs elsewhere where they could learn new things instead of just exploiting what they already knew, month in and month out. They were fighting learned helplessness, which we now know is bad for physical health. And there were many, many job options for programmers with their experience and talent. Haddon had won the old war for talent by attracting these incredible people, but he was losing the new war for talent by failing to keep their seeking systems activated.

To some, it may seem counterintuitive that it can be bad for people to focus on outcomes and measurements of performance. But the phenomenon that Toby Haddon was watching unfold is the same exposed by Amy Edmondson in the open-heart surgery teams. When agility and innovation are called for, it's better for employees to frame their goals around learning (e.g., developing a new set of skills; mastering a new situation) rather than performance outcomes (e.g., hitting results targets; proving competence).

Don Vandewalle and his colleagues found similar results when they asked sales reps to fill out a survey when a new product had been introduced. Salespeople answered one set of questions about learning goals (for example, "Learning how to be a better salesperson is of fundamental importance to me.") They answered another set of questions oriented toward achievement goals (such as "I spend a lot of time thinking about how my performance compares with other salespeople's."). Later, after the product promotion was over, the researchers looked at how many units each salesperson had sold. It turned out that employees with a learning mindset sold significantly more of the new product: in fact, simply knowing salespeople's mindset let the researchers predict 11 percent of the sales that were made.[2]

A raft of studies over the last twenty years align with Vandewalle's and Edmondson's findings.[3] Simply put, learning goals are more effective at improving performance in changing environments where innovation is important. This is because they draw our attention away from the end result and encourage us instead to use our curiosity and discover novel strategies.

Capitalizing on Creativity

To activate employees' seeking systems and prompt a learning mindset at Dealogic, Haddon and I borrowed concepts from 3M's "bootleg time" and Atlassian's ShipIt program.[4] These are essentially programs that give people free time to experiment with their own projects and interests, a little like Google's "20 percent time" idea (more on that later).

In our experiment at Dealogic, we gave forty engineers in London and Budapest twenty-four hours to work on whatever they wanted, with whomever they wanted. We encouraged, but did not demand, cross-discipline teams of, say, engineers and software architects. The only suggestion was that people should work on something connected with Dealogic and/or the technical stack under which they operate. Because less-technical people were involved, there was no requirement that the solution had to be coded. Then, after twenty-four hours, all project teams (sometimes comprising just one individual who had decided to work alone) would meet back and present to each other and to senior management (CEO, managing director, COO) what they had experimented with and what they had learned.

By the Wednesday of the event, teams submitted an idea they wanted to explore. These write-ups were very light, but they specified who was on the team, the general topic, and the scope of the experiment. Creative Capital ran from 2 p.m. on Thursday until close of business on Friday. The office space remained open for the full period, and food and drinks were provided on Thursday evening for anyone staying late. People were asked to stop working on their projects at 2 p.m. on Friday, and the remainder of the afternoon focused on presentations from each project.

As Antony Trapp, a Dealogic leader who helped manage the event internally, described it:

> People seemed excited by the event. In the end, only three
> people out of more than forty people chose not to be
> involved. The atmosphere in the team area on Friday, as the
> deadline was approaching, was pretty electric. Some of the
> presentations were very smart and funny and helped create
> a very positive atmosphere with great energy. Every single
> project was applauded by the audience, so there was a
> strong sense that everyone felt recognized for their efforts.

A number of nonprogrammers approached me just prior to the presentations wanting to be involved next time. It seemed to generate a buzz in the office as a whole.

We called the project "Creative Capital" because if the management team liked the direction of an experiment, they invested into the team. But they didn't invest money; they invested *time*. Overall, forty percent of the projects received some level of time funding, and were moving forward the next week. For example, Lipot's team, which had created the notification system to send news out to clients' phones, already demonstrated some functionality. That team received two weeks to play the ideas out into an application. The team really threw themselves into it, and two weeks later they delivered a fully functioning app that worked on three phone platforms, and also had dealt with the security issues. This investment of time meant that the team's own experiment in learning became part of their "real job." To put it another way, they got paid to pursue their own innovations.

Another team created a refreshed version of a website showing the status of test systems. This idea got traction even more quickly—their concept was in the process of going live the Monday following the event. As of the Wednesday after the event, another project (around smart search) was already being included in a project. The same was true of promising ideas that needed further development. If management saw the potential in a person's idea, they might tell her to spend a half day per week pursuing her idea.

After the event, employees' were asked to fill in anonymous surveys. Their open-ended comments were very positive. Several showed the enthusiasm that can be activated by experimenting. One employee wrote, "It's been a great experience, and moved a lot of people from the 'grey weekdays.'" Another wrote, "This let us start to THINK and not just DO." Another employee said, "It was good to see that company cares about the individual ideas. Keep it up." A few weeks after the event, Trapp told me, "The atmosphere across the teams is better, and people certainly seem to be interacting in a more regular and positive sense."

By encouraging employees to experiment and explore new ideas, Dealogic activated their seeking systems, resulting in zest and intrinsic motivation. The result was more exploration and creativity, which led to new ideas. In fact, Haddon told me, "The ideas coming out of these experiments have worked out much better than the dedicated R&D department we set up." As Trapp observed about Creative Capital: "You show to the whole company what can be accomplished in twenty-four hours . . . we sometimes forget the basics. You have to focus on just the vital elements of the thing you're creating. And then you see what people accomplish and you say 'If we can do *that* in twenty-four hours, why can't we do this with other things? We're better than this.' It's a way to inspire ourselves."

Some of the new ideas and products could be considered great outcomes. But even more broadly, and more importantly, the Dealogic experiment showed me that an innovation culture must be nurtured. It's not enough to hire creative and highly motivated people; that's the old war for talent. As a leader, you also have to activate people's seeking systems to ignite their intrinsic motivation and creativity.

Keep the Momentum Going

Initiatives such as Creative Capital are great ways to energize employees and maximize their creative energy. This helps create an innovation culture in part because leaders are *modeling* experimentation and learning. At Dealogic, Toby Haddon and Antony Trapp tried something new, even though they didn't know exactly where it would go or how it would work. Right off the bat, this uncertainty and experimentation created a kind of excitement that is hard to produce when you know exactly how an initiative is going to play out.

But, to be honest, it's difficult to keep the momentum going.

We learned this lesson at Dealogic. Given the success of the first event, the leaders decided to "scale up" and hold four Creative Capital sessions per year. This seemed perfectly reasonable, given the success of the first event. Nevertheless, enthusiasm began to wane. Irfan Ikram, who had become the champion of the initiative, told me: "After three of four Creative Capital sessions, the event had generally lost its sparkle among a lot of staff members. Most people seemed disinterested in it due to factors ranging from the projects not going anywhere to it being hard to come up with an idea every quarter."

Essentially, the initiative became just another business process. Employees started to grow weary of "forced freedom." This resulted in fewer and fewer participants.

The lesson here—and the challenge—is that play can't be contrived. It can be primed, but at the same time it has to be organic. It can take trial and error to find the right balance.

To address this issue, Dealogic's management team tried to tie the event to a specific product challenge. Ironically, this took even more play out of the process for employees, and was even less successful. Ikram told me:

> We outlined several business problems that participants could pick from or engage with a product team member to build . . . This we thought would help reduce the burden on coming up with ideas from everyone and at the same time tie the event to product-based ideas which had a much higher chance of being taken forward (which was a big complaint). This completely backfired . . . the feedback was resounding that the event had just become too restrictive and the few people who entered started stepping away. People wanted freedom of choice.

After meeting with groups of employees at each location, Ikram found a way that Creative Capital works best, at least at the time of writing this book. The event currently has its highest-ever participation rates across all regions. In New York, for example, the most recent event led to 30 percent more participation than in any other Creative Capital event. Some of the key adjustments included:

- Frequency. The event now runs twice a year, which gives employees enough time to think of ideas for the next event (a year in technology is a long time).

- Local focus. Dealogic established a steering group for each location's event, and split each event so every region would run at a different time, allowing the steering group to focus.

- Judging panel. Based on feedback that the judging wasn't transparent, Dealogic created easy-to-follow criteria and a five-person judging panel.

- Prizes. Even though intrinsic motivation was the goal, things went better when Dealogic rewarded the top three ideas with a £50 gift voucher, as opposed to only the top one.

So the leadership team had to play with different elements of the event to keep it fresh. It's working great again for now, but of course they'll need to keep experimenting with experimenting.

Changing the Game

Dealogic's Creative Capital program is a micro version of a more comprehensive practice at Shell Oil.[5] With over $100 billion in revenues, over 100,000 employees, and nearly a hundred years of tradition, Shell is not the type of organization where you'd expect to find entrepreneurial zest. In fact, one employee compared Shell to a maze of hundred-foot-high brick walls: access to capital is tightly controlled, investment hurdles are daunting, and radical ideas either die or move very slowly.[6]

Tim Warren, director of Research and Technical Services, set out to prompt innovation in the technical function of Shell's exploration business. To trigger innovative new ideas, Tim tried to encourage employees to spend some their time working on "bootleg projects" and "nonlinear ideas" that are outside their normal job scope. He said the results were underwhelming—almost everybody was stuck in predictable, confined patterns of work. Which is not surprising when the drive to meet normal operations and hit existing KPIs consumes all our time and energy.

So Warren scaled things up by creating a small panel of employees with the authority to allocate $20 million to rule-breaking, game-changing ideas. The new practice, called GameChanger, started with the assumption that ideas could come from anywhere across the company, and did not need to come from a certain department. Then Tim waited for the avalanche of game-changing, revolutionary ideas. The avalanche was more like a trickle. The fact that even $20 million was not enough to break people out of their learned helplessness shows how shut off employees were to exploration.

But Warren didn't give up. With the help of a consulting firm, he built a three-day Ideation Lab. Seventy-two would-be entrepreneurs showed up. Lots of them were employees whom no one suspected of harboring an entrepreneurial impulse. In the lab, these participants went through a process of discovery, focusing on disruptive changes in the external environment (both within and beyond Shell's industry). They worked on how Shell might harness this disruption, overturning the normal rules of the game.

Going through this process turned participants on; in fact, because emotions are contagious, their enthusiasm created some curiosity in nonparticipants. So many people started checking in on the excitement in the lab that "the doors to the conference room had to be locked to keep the overwhelming number of 'gate crashers' out."[7]

By day 2, the group had unleashed 240 new ideas. Some of the concepts were entirely new businesses, while others were new approaches within existing businesses. Like the Creative Capital program, the potential business concepts were then released into a kind of open market. Rather than organizational leaders funding people with time, however, at Shell, the investments were made by other Ideation Lab participants. These individuals responded to the "gravitational pull" that attracted them to one idea rather than another. It was self-selection at work. This means that in the end, groups of three to four individuals clustered around the business concept that most appealed to them.

But, as we will see later with Google, too much freedom and too many new ideas can cause their own problems. New ideas need a way to turn into reality and not just die on the vine. Tim Warren and his colleagues had worked hard to create an innovation space within Shell, and it paid off. A group of employees' seeking systems had been activated, and the employees were ready to experiment with something that excited them. They were unclear what to do next, however. What Warren and his panel recognized was that "permission to innovate" is necessary, but not sufficient. What they needed next was a process to refine people's promising ideas through a business plan phase.

To accomplish this goal, they built an Action Lab, designed as an intensive five-day experience to help people develop their ideas into compelling venture plans for launching new businesses. For this, the program moved away from Shell's Hague headquarters to a fourteenth-century castle in Maastricht, Belgium. Here, Tim and his colleagues brought videoconferencing, video production technology, graphic artists, a film crew, venture capitalists, entrepreneurs, and marketing gurus together under one roof. It was a large investment in an innovation hothouse—an immersive, resource-rich environment designed to inspire and to incubate new ventures. The teams of Shell employees learned how to scope out the boundaries of their ideas, identify partnerships, determine the competitive advantage of their ideas, and calculate the financial implications. They were coached in developing hundred-day action plans, which formulated ways to learn fast—devising low-cost, low-risk ways of prototyping and testing their ideas in the marketplace. We saw a similar process in the white-goods plant that implemented lean manufacturing (chapter 5).

The Shell teams also were coached to bring their ideas to life using storytelling. They worked with the graphic artists who helped them create product prototypes, and they worked with video film crews to create short-length infomercials to communicate the essence of their ventures. At the conclusion of the week, each team presented a story to a venture board (the GameChanger panel, along with a sampling of senior Shell executives and leaders who knew how to fund late-stage technology commercialization). Four teams received six-month funding to put them on a path toward full-fledged business plans.

GameChanger has been a huge investment in innovation. The panel meets weekly to discuss new submissions, and its members serve as coaches and advocates for prospective innovators. Any employee with a promising idea is invited to give a ten-minute pitch to the panel, followed by a fifteen-minute Q&A session. If members agree that the idea has potential, the employee returns for a second round of discussions with a broader group of company experts whose knowledge or support may be important to the success of the proposed venture. Ideas that get a green light often receive funding—on average $100,000, but sometimes as much as $600,000—within eight or ten days. Each project goes through a proof-of-concept review, in which the team must demonstrate that its plan is indeed workable in order to win further funding. This review typically marks the point at which the GameChanger panel helps successful ventures find a permanent home inside Shell.

Of course, many projects are not funded, and not all of the projects that were funded worked from a commercial perspective. Like Dealogic's Creative Capital program, the more important point is that the program triggered experimentation and learning, and energized people to play to their personal interests and unique strengths instead of feeling learned helplessness.

Both the employees and the corporation win when employees feel energized to innovate in this way. And about a quarter of GameChanger's ventures have found homes in a Shell operating unit or in one of the company's various growth initiatives, while others have been carried forward as R&D projects. The remainder have been wound down and written off as useful experiments. As described to me by my colleague Julian Birkinshaw, a professor of strategy at London Business School: "I think that GameChanger provides a process for the sort of hunch-based research that scientists demand, but which hard-pressed business sponsors are loath to underwrite."

Getting the Balance Right

In this chapter, we saw different approaches for using experimentation and playing to personal strengths as a way to switch on employees' seeking systems within their organizational frame. We saw how people gained enthusiasm and commitment and became more creative. Work started to feel more like real life to these individuals. This is where humanism fuels a sustained competitive advantage.

But getting the balance right between the freedom and the frame is not always easy. As we saw with both Dealogic and Shell, experimentation itself is something that needs to be experimented with to get it right.

Google's "20 percent time" policy is probably the most famous example. It's widely known that Google engineers were encouraged to spend 20 percent of their time on personal projects. The policy resulted in some successful products such as Gmail, AdSense, and Google Talk. Founders Larry Page and Sergey Brin even highlighted the importance of this management method in a founders' IPO letter to prospective investors in 2004: "We encourage our employees, in addition to their regular projects, to spend 20 percent of their time working on what they think will most benefit Google . . . This empowers them to be more creative and innovative."[8]

But in 2013, Google cut back on this policy. According to the engineers, managers clamped down on staff taking their 20 percent time to keep their teams from falling behind in Google's internal productivity rankings. Managers were judged on the productivity of their teams, so time spent on the personal projects hurt them.[9] The result has been more tightly-targeted innovation activities with more top-down framing of focus areas that spur the bottom-up innovations.[10] As we saw in chapter 2, when companies like Google go from startup to large global business, they look to exploit more and innovate less so that they can derive more value from existing products. This requires a more operational focus on existing product lines. The frame gets smaller, and freedom to innovate shrinks.

It would be easy to condemn Google's decision to cut its 20 percent policy as a shortsighted hampering of employees' seeking systems—especially when the policy had a track record of proven innovations. However, remember the balance: freedom must be within the frame of what an organization needs to deliver. Twenty percent time might balance well when you have a hundred engineers, and every few months a good idea emerges that attracts other employees and the idea becomes a movement.[11] No doubt, this freedom to invent would be like a jolt of electricity to those employees' seeking systems, fueling their zest and driving them to do more and more. However, the same freedom may not fit into an organizational frame with 20,800 engineers. Encouraging that many people to spend 20 percent of their time in discovery led to "too many arrows with not enough wood behind them," as Google CEO Larry Page explained.[12] Perhaps letting a thousand flowers bloom ended up with a whole new bed of flowers growing each week, yet none of them being harvested and put to good use.

The tension between freedom and frame is very real in both directions. Most large organizations err on the side of too much frame and not enough freedom, but perhaps 20 percent was too much freedom. I'm proposing that leaders need to encourage enough freedom so that the frame does not become an iron cage, and employees feel they can experiment and learn.

The goal of this book is not to have you copy the specific ideas that these leaders used. If you can use them, great, but of course a good idea depends on industry or country culture. The most important takeaway is understanding the biological seeking system that all employees possess, and then investing to activate it. This happens when we create work environments where employees feel encouraged to play around with their intrinsic interests and personal strengths within the frame of the organizational demands.

This is not how personnel policies originally were set up under scientific management. This is not how hierarchical "power" usually works in organizations, and this is not how most of us have been taught to lead change. So, to close off this section of the book, in chapter 7 we look at our fundamental beliefs about what leadership is "for," and how these beliefs affect our ability to trigger employees' seeking systems.

CHAPTER 7

HUMBLE LEADERSHIP AND EMPLOYEES' SEEKING SYSTEMS

6:30 in the morning, still dark outside. The alarm squawks at Zhang Min and her eight-hundred-square-foot apartment in Chengdu, China, just outside of Chongqing Nan'an. She'd love to eat something before she leaves, but she needs to make the train to get to work at Standard Chartered Bank, the British multinational financial services company.

Soon after, she is squeezing through the forest of arms and torsos toward the train door at Nanping station, just like the other 900,000 people using this stop today. Her belly grumbling, she wishes she'd eaten a boiled egg on the way to the station. It's hot—almost 85°F. It's going up to 104° today.

Getting out of the train, she makes her way over to the Chong-qing Wanda Shopping Centre with ten thousand other employees. The breeze along Jiangnan Avenue outside feels good on her face, which is damp from the train. As she approaches the front door of the branch, she can tell something is going on. There are too many people in the main lobby for this early in the day. She checks her watch and quickens her step. The branch doesn't even open for another twenty minutes; they can't be customers.

Some unfamiliar faces—men in red aprons holding trays—seem to be in the middle of everyone. "Did I miss an announce-ment?" Zhang Min wonders. She shoots a questioning look to Mai with raised eyebrows, but Mai only holds up a juice and smiles.

Still confused, Zhang Min tries to squeeze through the crowd to get to her desk, but an aproned man smiles and hands her a drink and a warm box. He introduces himself as Jungkiu Choi, the new head of Consumer Banking. Zhang Min's heart jumps and she hopes her fear doesn't show in her eyes. "But we aren't ready yet!" she says, wondering how her branch manager messed up this visit.

Each year, the Standard Chartered Bank executives make a pilgrimage to each of its branches. But their visits were always announced in advance, giving the employees time to prep. Last year, Zhang Min put in about twenty extra hours, cleaning and painting the public areas, making all the filing systems neat, pre-paring the PowerPoint presentations. It was hard keeping up with her usual customer relationship work during this preparation, but the branch manager was intent on showing the executives a "clean face." Now, the executives were here in the building, and Zhang

Min and her colleagues had done nothing to make their visit a good one. Her stress levels rise.

No one else seems anxious, though. Looking around, Zhang Min sees several of her coworkers are laughing, smiling, and eating with the head of the region, who is also serving food, wearing a red apron. Zhang Min can't believe what she's seeing. Last year, she stood waiting outside in the burning sun with drinks, sweating all the way through her blue blazer, to greet the executives. By the time they arrived, two and half hours late, the ice had melted. And, after all the overtime she had worked to prepare for their visit, she felt melted too.

Today, after everyone has arrived and has had some breakfast, Jungkiu asks Zhang Min and eight other branch employees to join him in a "morning huddle." In a small meeting room, he tells the team that he would like to discuss what problems are blocking great customer service at the bank. His job, he tells them, is to try and eliminate those problems, and he'll do everything in his power to help them.

As Zhang Min finishes her pastry, she can't believe what she's hearing. Never before has an executive asked her and her colleagues how they might solve problems. At last year's visit, for example, the team wanted to propose extending the branch's hours of operation. But after serving the executives their meal, presenting their extensive PowerPoint demonstration, and giving their well-scripted Q&A session for the leaders, they ran out of time to talk about what mattered most to the branch employees. Zhang Min shut off after that. "It's just a job; it pays the bills," she thought, and she began to keep her ideas to herself.

Servant Leadership

When Jungkiu Choi moved to China from Singapore as the new head of Consumer Banking, he learned that one of the cultural expectations of his job was to visit the branches as a "superior commander." When the previous consumer banking heads made branch visits, they emphasized the organization's hierarchy and their power. This put a lot of pressure on the branches, as staff would spend weeks anxiously preparing for the visit.

Jungkiu Choi didn't see the point. In his view, this practice put a lot of undue stress on the employees, so the visits weren't productive. He saw the leader's role as something quite different—imposing authority was not the way to engage his employees in change. In this chapter, we will see that when leaders are trying to activate employees' seeking systems with experimentation, being humble and trying to learn from employees is more effective than emphasizing hierarchy. As Gary Hamel once told me: "Show me what you can get done when you have no budget and no authority. That's how you know you're a leader."

As one of his first actions in his new role, Jungkiu decided to lessen the burden of executive visits to branches. Along with his team, he instituted three key changes from which everything else flowed: (1) branches would not be notified of the visit; (2) the visit would start with executives serving breakfast rather than making the branch employees wait for executives to arrive and then serve them meals; and (3) the executives would hold "huddles" and ask how they could help employees improve their branches. Jungkiu's trip to the Chongqing Nan'an branch, where Zhang Min worked, was his first official visit. Along with the head of Consumer Banking, head of Distribution, and head of the region, he arrived early and greeted employees with breakfast as they arrived at work. Many of the employees were very surprised and initially did not know how to react. But after they received their breakfasts and talked about their ideas for improving how the branch worked, they were energized. As one employee wrote in the company bulletin: "Jungkiu believes if we want to treat our customers well, we must treat and surprise the frontline as well. He believes in servant leadership. Jungkiu, Victor, Alan, and Marco are dressed in aprons and are serving our staff breakfast. Never seen such charismatic waiters, right?"

I suggest that Jungkiu's new approach worked because it tamped down employees' fear and encouraged ideation and self-expression, which activated their seeking systems. The result? Jungkiu unleashed lots of good ideas and enthusiasm for improvements.

Although he was achieving good results at the branches, putting this idea into practice wasn't easy. When he first announced his new approach, Jungkiu had had trouble convincing other leaders. Many of the executive team members did not support the idea. They told him: "In China, the boss should retain mystique and cannot be too close to the front."

Jungkiu worried about this attitude. He told me: "The fundamental question I discussed with my executive team was whether the job of a business leader is the "emperor"—someone who rules above you—or the "facilitator"—a vision shaper and bottleneck remover. If we define ourselves as the former, the leader should keep the distance and retain mystique. If we define ourselves as the latter, the leader should be humble, close, and open."

Over the course of one year, Jungkiu visited over eighty branches in twenty-five cities. His consistency helped convince employees who were skeptical at first that the visits were a "one-off." The huddles, focused on employees' ideas and experiments, were interactive sessions that included role-play around customer conversations (and usually included laughter and joking). Some of the role-plays focused on the new customer financial planning tools, and seeing how they actually worked and where they were difficult.

In this way, the new branch visits were work-focused, but they were fueled by positive emotions created by the seeking system. The openness of the huddle exposed the most simple of pain points that Jungkiu could easily help solve (for example, training for the new bank systems, or making upgrades to computer memory so that the old computers could handle the new software).

Jungkiu told me that repeating the breakfasts and listening sessions was important because when he took the job, branch employees' anxiety about management was as high as their trust was low. Previous banking heads came to the branches after receiving their promotion and tried to squeeze performance mainly through exploitation—cost reduction and short-term tactics—before moving on to their next job. Jungkiu was the eleventh consumer banking head in ten years, and many of the employees' ideas and frontline pain points had simply not been addressed by previous leaders.

For example, one of the Shanghai branches was inside of a shopping mall. In the huddle, employees asked Jungkiu if they could open and close the same times as the mall's operating hours (rather than the typical branch operating hours). This would include opening on the weekends. The team *wanted* to experiment with working on the weekends. Within a few months, this branch's weekend income generation surpassed its entire weekday income. This was not an idea that Jungkiu had even imagined.

Jungkiu also found that encouraging experimentation increased peoples' confidence to innovate, leading to more enthusiasm and commitment. He told me: "If you let a call center solve a small customer dispute, without asking for any reports, I find they manage as if they are the owners of the bank. If you impose too many processes and rules on the call, they mechanically follow the processes and rules, without concerning themselves with benefits or costs to the bank or the customers."

This goes back to the importance of letting employees find the freedom within the organizational frame. And, Jungkiu's experience also echoes what we saw in the Italian white-goods facility in chapter 5 and the Dealogic example in chapter 6: the seeking system generates enthusiasm and an intrinsic motivation to understand and explore, rather than an extrinsic motivation to simply follow existing approaches.

At another branch in Ningbo, the team asked if they could try hiring more direct sales staff. They described their opportunities to serve customers and why they believed they could hire top-quality talent. The branch manager told Jungkiu, "Ningbo is one of the richest cities in China, with many young and upwardly mobile people traveling there from overseas to study. But there are not many multinational companies these people can work for. So we could easily hire some of the best people on the market."

It was a good idea, but it entailed a lot of work. The branch employees' enthusiasm energized them to pull it off. Direct sales productivity at the Ningbo branch became the highest in the entire China network. This was not Jungkiu's idea: this was him activating people's seeking systems and then helping them try out their ideas.

As momentum grew for the new type of branch visits, employees started uploading pictures they took during the sessions to Weibo (the Chinese version of Facebook + Twitter). As an informal (and unpredicted) forum of communication, Weibo turned out to be far more effective than the more formal medium of company newsletters.

Jungkiu's approach to branch visits is another example of a wise intervention, which we learned about in chapter 3: small but potent changes, like removing the anxiety around the branch visits and replacing it with serving breakfast and talking about new ideas, led to very large-scale changes, including a culture of ownership and innovation.

In addition to increasing employees' zest and activating their seeking systems, these experiments paid off in terms of company performance. For example, customer satisfaction increased by 54 percent during the two-year period of Jungkiu's humble leadership. Complaints from customers were reduced by 29 percent during the same period. The employee attrition ratio had been the highest among all the foreign banks in China; during the same period, it was reduced to the lowest among all foreign banks in China.

As Jungkiu said, "I have found that people do not move much by KPIs and reward/penalty. These cause small changes. People move in larger ways by noble purpose, emotional connection, experimenting with new things, and leading by example."

To put it another way, leaders should see themselves as humble servants.

Why Does Humble Leadership Work?

To prompt employees' curiosity and learning through experimentation, a leader can start with the humble purpose of serving others and being open to learning from employees. Bradley Owens, a professor at Brigham Young University, and David Hekman, a professor at University of Colorado, conducted fifty-five in-depth interviews with leaders from a wide variety of contexts. They found that when leaders express feelings of uncertainty and humility, and share their own developmental journeys, they end up encouraging a learning mindset in others.[1]

Ironically, humble leadership works not by demanding perfection, but its opposite—by showing that humans are never perfect and must explore, fail, and practice in order to learn and improve. This is the phenomenon we saw with the surgeons in chapter 5, who successfully learned how to conduct less-invasive heart surgery not by demanding perfection immediately but by being open to the team's needs and focusing the team on learning and practice.

Some leaders, as we saw initially with some of Jungkiu's colleagues, are hesitant to follow a humble leadership model. When I present Jungkiu's case to leadership teams, their intuition is that his humble actions of listening to employees and helping them experiment do not seem how "real leaders" should act, especially in Far East cultures. They find his story interesting, but then ask, "Does humility really work? When does it backfire?"

I would argue that "bureaucratic leadership," with its reliance on certainty, decisiveness, and positional power, is detrimental because it ramps up people's fear systems, shuts down positive emotions, and stifles the drive to experiment and learn. This so-called executive disease is common because power changes how leaders view other people—research shows that power causes people to see others as a means to their ends rather than as intelligent humans with ideas and emotions.[2] In organizational life, power can result in arrogance and self-importance, and executives too often use their power to bully and frighten employees into compliance.[3]

Employees' fear of powerful leaders also creates sycophants, who buffer leaders from real information. This makes leaders more and more detached from the reality of work, pain points, and customers. Unfortunately, this situation feels really good to executives themselves. As they become very comfortable, they usually set out to protect and preserve their ego and power.[4] Trying to learn from employees—and helping employees experiment and learn with new approaches to work—is not even in their picture.

Remember the concept of learned helplessness from chapter 2—the experiment in which dogs receiving repeated electric shocks no longer tried to escape their pain? Here's a thought: arrogance is often a form of learned helplessness. We all know that learning can only start if we are willing to acknowledge that we don't know everything. But what happens if people work in an environment where admitting they don't know everything is viewed by others as a sign of weakness, and punished? This happens a lot in banking environments, for example, where people pretend to be "masters of the universe."

What if you are a leader who is punished for acknowledging that others have better information than you? It makes you pretend to know better, when in fact you don't. In this sense, arrogance is a defense system that prevents people from having to admit they don't know. Try to put yourself in this banker's shoes: "If I admit lack of knowledge, then I am punished, so I can't learn. I am rewarded for confidently faking that I know best when I don't."

This dynamic is important because it stifles learning and innovation for people in power. Not knowing is ridiculed and punished, while acting confident (even when ignorant) is respected and rewarded. If we are repeatedly hurt for learning and listening to others' ideas, arrogance becomes a form of learned helplessness. What emerges is an arrogant culture, and learning stops. These cultures tell employees: "Supervisors don't want your new ideas or attempts to innovate." Maybe this is OK if your company doesn't need to change much and you can tell people what to do; it's disastrous if you need agility and employee innovation.

Although it is hard for us all to stay humble and not preen our egos in the face of bureaucratic power, science clearly shows that humble, servant-oriented leadership works. A wave of well-conducted research investigations over the last ten years have demonstrated that humble, servant-oriented leadership improves performance at the individual, team, and organizational level.[5] It's not that power in leadership is a bad thing, per se. Humans, like many other social species, look for leadership from those who do impressive things that help us or inspire us. This makes us *want* to follow them. But during the Industrial Revolution, leadership got entangled with hierarchy—leaders were assigned power that was not earned. Humble leadership is more natural, because humble leaders help other people seek their potential, and experiment toward that potential. This is a gift that makes other people want to give back, and want to follow.[6]

Here is what we know: humble leaders help people move toward their full potential, growing and trying new ideas on the job. This works partly because humble leaders model how to grow to their followers. Rather than just talking about the importance of learning and experimenting, humble leaders model how to develop—by acknowledging mistakes and limitations and being open to listening, observing, and learning-by-doing. We saw this with Jungkiu at Standard Chartered Bank, with Dealogic's Creative Capital experiments, and KLM's social media experiments.

When an organization needs to adapt and adjust frequently, humility allows both leaders and followers to be more receptive to new ideas, criticism, or changes in the external environment. As one leader said, "Failure finds its grace in adjustment."

Leader humility is an essential tool in the new war for talent. Employees bring more of themselves to work when their leaders place a priority on activating their seeking systems—by providing tangible and emotional support to them as they explore new ways to improve themselves and their environments.

Delivering Creativity

Jungkiu's experiences at Standard Chartered Bank suggest that humble leadership can activate employees' seeking systems even when anxiety is high. But what about when employees have lapsed deep into learned helplessness?

Consider a UK food delivery business. Every morning, its drivers—called *roundsmen*—deliver essential groceries to customers. Early in the morning, hundreds of them load their trucks and bring milk and bread to more than 1 million customers.

Many of the drivers had worked there for fifteen to twenty years, and had long ago soured on management. As is often the case in organizations, the managers were not respectful of lower-level employees and their ideas. This is a sort of "creativity apartheid"—a class system that can emerge in organizations where white-collar employees believe themselves to be creative, while blue-collar employees are not. Over time, drivers became distrustful, shut off their seeking systems at work, and negative emotions dominated. You could hear it in the roundsmen's cynical banter about management as they loaded up their trucks in the depot before delivery runs.

As the company's profits were being pinched by big delivery companies like Ocado, the disconnect between management and drivers became a bigger problem. With years of a shrinking customer base and limited possibilities for growth, the only way the company could survive was through excellent customer service. However, the attitudes and behaviors of its employees were making it difficult to deliver on this possibility. They were not keen on helping managers implement organizational change, even though it could preserve their own jobs.

The company hired Duncan Wardley, a director at PwC, to help it identify the key "moments that matter" for both customers and staff—key interactions that, if done well, have a disproportionate impact. Moments that matter are perfect for the wise interventions we learned about in chapter 3.

One of the most important interactions, Wardley and his team discovered, was the weekly "Roundsman's Debriefs" between a depot manager and a delivery person. These meetings happened once a week and lasted for fifteen minutes, sometimes less. The drivers certainly wanted them to be less.

It's not that the depot managers were bad people—for the most part, they were salt-of-the-earth types whose hearts were in the right place about organizational success. But they were old-school. Their methods for achieving better performance were authoritarian and paternalistic. They used dominance and anxiety to try and force better performance, and that tactic was all they knew.

These weekly Roundsman's Debriefs were essentially the depot managers' way of letting the drivers know that they were watching them and were recording their errors for punishment. In these meetings, the depot managers would literally go through a list of problems: customer complaints, missed deliveries, and the like. Some people called this "management-by-clipboard." The drivers felt like they were being treated like naughty children. They would literally stand in front of the depot manager, who was seated at his desk, as they were grilled about a dirty uniform.

This is where the leadership mindset change was needed to ignite employees' seeking systems. Remember what we learned about humble leadership: it is based *on serving employees*. Because management is an overhead cost, managers do not create value unless they are serving the employees who create the value. In that light, it's obvious that the existing format of the Rounds-man's Debrief was not a quest to learn and help solve problems. It was, at best, a parent-child conversation. In fact, to drivers it did not even feel they were part of a human interaction, but a tick-box exercise designed to catch them out. Each debrief hurt the relationship a little more, increasing the conflict between people who needed to be partners. The debriefs demoralized, belittled, and angered the very drivers whom management needed to deliver world-class service. The strategy and the execution were not joining up.

Worse, since the Roundsman's Debriefs were usually one-way conversations, the managers were preventing themselves from receiving on-the-ground feedback from drivers. For example, some of so-called "mistakes" that drivers were making were actually innovations they had created to streamline processes and still deliver everything on time. In a more collaborative setting, these innovations would have come to light and would have helped the company deliver better customer service. They could have been trails into the root cause of the company's delivery problems.

Wardley's dream was to transform these hated meetings into fifteen-minute conversations where the primary focus would be finding and experimenting with new ways to deliver excellent customer service. The goal was for the meetings to be well-run, two-way, problem-solving dialogues where the depot managers learned where they could help. In turn, the roundsmen would view them as positive, helpful conversations. These exchanges, in turn, could lead to positive impacts on the other "moments that matter," like a customer's initial delivery experience or finding new ways of reducing costs.

Given that negative emotions (including anger and anxiety) dominated the current culture, how could Wardley turn his dream into the roundsmen's reality?

PwC started with a small, wise intervention: take the standard fifteen-minute format for the weekly meeting and have managers start the meeting with a basic servant leadership question: "How can I help you deliver excellent service?"

PwC ran a coaching program to support depot managers in getting this right. The program focused on how to conduct such conversations, and how to identify the rich information and ideas that could be uncovered through this new style of interacting. After the new approach was introduced to the depot managers, they role-played the process with the consultants. Senior leadership also role-played to model the learning process, and to send the message "this really, actually is important to us."

The depot managers clearly did not think this new meeting format would change anything. And they said so. One of the depot managers told Wardley: "Listen, I will do this, but I know these drivers, and it will not work." The new approach went against some of their most basic assumptions about how to manage and motivate the roundsmen.

To assuage their fears, PwC spent time with them, observing their conversations with delivery people, helping them to understand what they needed to do differently and coaching them through the entire discussion.

It was slow going at first. Drivers' dislike of managers was high, and trust was low. But as depot managers kept asking "How can I help you deliver excellent service?" some drivers eventually offered suggestions: "If you want clean uniforms when we deliver, don't make us wear our clean uniforms when we load up the vehicles," one driver told his manager. In response, the manager bought coveralls that drivers could wear as they loaded the trucks. Changes like these, however small, built trust, and drivers suggested other ideas. For example, one driver suggested new products like "Gogurts" and fun string cheese that parents could get delivered early and pop into their kids' lunches before school. Another driver thought of a way to report stock shortages more quickly so that customers were not left without the groceries they ordered.

Here we see a virtuous cycle: each positive step led to another, bigger positive step. One driver's successful change activated three other drivers who saw that change was possible. As shown in Owens and Hekman's research on humble leadership, the leaders needed to model serving employees so that employees would serve customers.[7] For drivers, it felt good to express and get some of their ideas in place—ideas they had locked away for many years as they shut off their seeking systems and allowed negative emotions to dominate.

As we saw with the assembly workers in the Italian white-goods facility, the drivers' seeking systems were activated because management listened to their ideas and took action, allowing zest and enthusiasm to push negative emotions into submission. According to one area manager: "The management style of the depot managers changed beyond recognition. They have developed a mutually respectful working relationship with the delivery people."

Even the most skeptical depot managers were impressed. What seemed like an incredibly small and simple change—opening the once-a-week meeting with a new question—culminated in real and important changes. When putting a wise intervention into place, it is important not to expect huge changes all at once. To overcome the learned helplessness that has built up for decades, small ideas have to be nurtured and developed. So the first few innovations and suggestions are likely to be small steps.

For the food delivery company, the ideas for improvements kept coming in. One driver came in with five pages of handwritten notes. Another driver suggested delivering Amazon and other parcels while they were on their runs. Another proposed dry-cleaning delivery services.

Leaders often do not see the true value of their charges, especially "lower-level" workers: drivers, call-center operators, mechanics, assembly people. But when leaders are humble, show respect, and ask how they can help employees do their work better, the outcomes can be outstanding. And even more important than better company results, humble leaders get to act like better human beings. They get to treat other people as they would like their own family to be treated.

Wardley and his team implemented a wise intervention. A single question. But it signaled a different leadership philosophy and led to very different conversations. This intervention shows the essence of *appreciative inquiry*, which breaks the cycle of depersonalization that shuts off employees' personal creativity.[8] As described in chapter 3, small changes like this can have hidden leverage when they focus on an emotionally vulnerable interaction, because it changes the basic story people tell themselves. As the roundsmen got credit for their ideas and saw them put into place, they grew more willing to offer more ideas, which made the depot managers more impressed and more respectful, which increased the roundsmen's willingness to give ideas, and so on.

As the roundsmen's seeking systems kicked in, the company got so many ideas about how to delight its customers that the bigger problem became how to deal with all the ideas. In the end, PwC helped managers segment the ideas into cost and benefit. They worked on implementing the simple, easy, and cheap ones (wear aprons over the uniforms) and making others into requests for capital (deliver wider range of products).

After a few weeks, the depot manager who had disputed the plan said, "I thought I knew these roundsmen. I've had to eat so much humble pie over last two weeks I've put on two stone [twenty-eight pounds]!" Another told Wardley, "There is a tangible difference. I simply wouldn't have believed it if I hadn't seen it with my own eyes."

Often, what causes big changes to happen and to stick is not logical. It's emotional. Wardley told me something that matched Jungkiu's words: "Real change is not achieved by simply offering rewards or appealing to people's reason. Instead, you have to tap into people's emotions. This means engaging with them in a different way—engaging with their sense of meaning and their intrinsic desire for self-expression."

An area manager summarized what a difference this made: "We really thought that we knew our delivery people inside out, but we've realized that there was a lot we were missing. Our weekly customer conversation meetings are now more interactive and the conversations are more honest and adult in their approach. It's hard to put into words the changes we are seeing."

It's pretty common for leaders to say that people don't like change. And many courses on leading change are dedicated to "overcoming employee resistance." I find it helpful to think about it the opposite way: people are really *good* at change.

Compared with all the other animals, humans are the ones *doing* all the change. When you look at our species' behavior relative to the others, we're the change animals. This seems to be the outcome when our seeking systems (which other mammals share) teams up with the prefrontal cortex (the new part of our brain that lets us simulate the future, which other mammals don't share).[9] Put these two parts of the brains together, and humans are biologically wired for innovation and change.

For example, we're not supposed to fly. Think about the other animals that don't have wings. What do they do? That's right: they just walk around. They take what is on offer from the world, and they get on with it. That is not how the human species acts. We just don't accept what the world has on offer. Remember, the world did not foist smartphones and artificial intelligence and blockchain technology onto us. The world is not doing this to us; we are doing this to ourselves. Thinking back to the increasing pace of innovation described in chapter 2, it's clear that the human animal is built for experimentation, learning, and innovation (see figure 7-1).

Now, we just need to learn how to activate these urges of the seeking system within the frame of organizational life. In both the UK food delivery example and the Chinese banking example,

FIGURE 7-1

Experimentation activates the seeking system

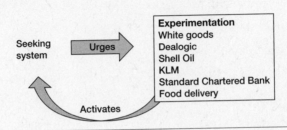

we saw how even disgruntled employees in learned helplessness mode can reactivate their seeking systems—when leaders are able to be humble, listen, and give them a chance to explore their environments and improve things. And the result is not just better products and services, it also is more enthusiasm and zest. People become alive at work.

PART IV

PURPOSE

CHAPTER 8

HELPING EMPLOYEES EXPERIENCE THE IMPACT OF THEIR WORK

Alex had every reason to like his job. The tire factory, which was located near his hometown in Russia, was new and modern and equipped with cutting-edge tools and technology.[1] The perks were great, too, like free tea and milk, and a great canteen with lots of good eating options. There was even a Finnish sauna.

On top of that, Alex genuinely thought that Nokian Tyres cared about him and his coworkers. The company provided free health services, funded a worker-led hockey team, and had sold Alex and his wife a company-built apartment for lower than market price.

But, at some point, Alex began to get tired of making tires. Not that there is anything wrong with making tires, of course—the world needs them, and someone has to make them. But it wasn't exactly the work that he had dreamed of doing when he was younger. Alex had pretty much mastered the role, and he yearned for work that was a little more . . . fulfilling.

Then Nokian introduced a new winter tire, and the marketing department organized a launch event in Ivalo, Finland. Supervisors from across the company were asked to nominate their best employees to go to the launch, and the general manager announced the invitees at the company New Year's Party. Alex was one of the chosen few.

When he heard his name called out, he was thrilled and a little bit frightened. He had never left Russia before or been on an airplane. But he was proud to be chosen by his supervisor to represent his group. He felt appreciated.

Alex experienced a lot of great things on his trip. For the first time, he saw Russia from the sky, and when he reached Finland, he witnessed the aurora borealis, which was beautiful and breathtaking. But there was more to the trip than sightseeing.

At the launch event, the organizers invited Janne Laitenen, a test driver for Nokian, to talk with the team and demonstrate some of his ice-driving techniques.[2] Laitenen, who holds the official Guinness World Record for fastest car on ice, talked about the winter tires and how they help him (and his car) perform at a high level.

After that, Laitenen invited Alex and the other Nokian employees to test out the tires, too, on a pure ice surface.

This was eye-opening for Alex. He had never really considered the end users of the product he was making. He was more concerned about the mechanics of his job: performing well and getting better. But the demonstration infused him with something new. He experienced the tangible effects of his work, and he was proud to be a part of a company that was making tires that could perform well in extreme conditions.

After returning to the facility, he felt more engaged in his work than ever before. Making tires seemed to take on a different meaning for him. In one sense, he was more tuned in to the excitement of tires and how they affected the driving experience. But even more broadly, he had a sense that the whole plant was pulling together to do one thing, to be the best in the world at what they do.

He felt a greater sense of purpose.

The Power in Purpose

From chapter 1, we know that, physically, the feeling of purpose is good for us—it affects our health and life expectancy. For example, a relatively small increase in sense of purpose—only a 1 standard deviation improvement—substantially reduces the risk of dying over the next decade.[3]

Purpose also is energizing, as in the case of Alex. It lights up our systems and gives us that jolt of dopamine. Alexander Ustavschikov, the general manager of the thousand-person Nokian facility, told me that the employees' feeling of purpose following the trip to Finland transformed the way they approached their work: "Tires became cool to them. It's very different than if we'd just have given them the €1,000 that the trip cost. Seeing the tires in action and connecting with what the other employees did—this changed the job for them. People feel more proud of the product they make, and of the company they work for, so they talk to their friends and relatives about the trip and the company. This even influences our brand."

Due to the seeking system, the feeling of purpose increases our enthusiasm, intrinsic motivation, and resilience. Remember, we also saw this with the Make-a-Wish Foundation (chapter 4), where part of the power of personalized job titles was helping employees focus on the core purpose of their work—creating joy for the families of sick children. The titles then served as a daily reminder of why employees worked there beyond the money.

Nokian is another case in point. When members of Alexander's team returned from Finland, he told me, "They brought a sense of mission and connectedness that was not there before the trip." These changes in attitudes and beliefs rippled back to the other employees, affecting the culture as a whole: "The trip changed people from the inside out, without me doing anything. I saw big changes in how people worked, how they acted in the facility. Workers started keeping their work areas more clean. Defects went down. Absenteeism dropped. The improvements in the facility were dramatic. Once people have felt the 'heart' of the company, they start to feel like they are not hired by the employer but truly feel like it is their own business."

What Alexander learned is that it can be much more powerful, more comprehensive, and less expensive to motivate people intrinsically (with purpose) rather than extrinsically (with incentives). When we have a personal experience that lets us develop a narrative and purpose about a certain activity, it activates our seeking system and we feel more zestful. The result? We engage ourselves even more in that activity. And, as we will see in chapter 9, the more we attach higher-order interpretations to our behaviors, the more we are willing to persevere with those behaviors through difficulty.

Is Creating Purpose Easy?

This all sounds great, right? Purpose is inexpensive motivation that feels good! But it's one thing to read about something in a business book and another to put the ideas into practice. This is particularly true of purpose.

Because purpose is personal and emotional, it is difficult for leaders to instill in others. It is even more tricky to sustain, even for people in altruistic organizations. For example, we all know schoolteachers and principals who have lost sight of the children and worry more about politics and break times. I have worked with many people in pharmaceutical companies, hospitals, and even the World Economic Forum who have lost the sense of purpose that originally attracted them to their jobs. Think about insurance companies. They work to ensure that people's families and most valued possessions are protected. But many of the people who work in insurance are disengaged and disconnected, with little sense of purpose in their work—including the leaders. If it can happen to people in these types of organizations, it can happen to anyone.

So how do we create the feeling of purpose and make sure it lasts? There are many ways to do this, as we'll see, but to have a shot at success, you need to help employees do two things: witness their impact on others and develop their own story about the *why* of their work. We'll deal with the first thing in this chapter and the second one in chapter 9.

Making It Personal

Imagine you're the manager of a call center for a college fundraiser and your goal is to improve the number of calls that employees make on their shifts, which in turn should increase donations. How would you do it?

Keep in mind that fundraising, even for a noble cause like funding scholarships for underprivileged students, can be a grueling, repetitive job. More than likely, your employees will be following a script and talking to people they've never met, most of whom will say no. It's a job that requires a lot of failure (about ten rejections for every successful call).

You could offer incentives, of course, creating a competition among employees for bonuses or gift cards. Or you could set SMART goals and implement more robust metrics. But as we've seen before, these often make employees anxious about hitting "number of calls made" targets rather than connecting in a meaningful way with potential donors. So they aren't the most effective approaches. To be successful, you'll need to activate your employees' seeking systems and help them gain a sense of purpose.

Adam Grant, who led the Make-A-Wish studies from chapter 4, has studied fundraisers too, and his research offers us insights on how this can be done.

Grant tried different interventions. In his first experiment, he separated fundraisers into three groups. The first was the control group, who performed their duties as usual. For the second group, Grant mixed things up. Before making calls, the fundraisers were taken into a break room for a ten-minute session with a manager, who read a one-page letter from a student beneficiary about how the scholarship had made a difference in his life.

The members of a third group were also presented with a letter, but then met the scholarship student, who thanked them in person. The call center workers then got a chance to ask him questions. For example, they asked about what classes he was taking, how he had obtained the scholarship, and what he was planning to do after graduating from college. There were no group hugs. It was not a tearful exchange—the student just thanked the call center workers for the work they do and answered their questions.

With these three conditions in place, Grant tracked employees' calls and revenues for four weeks. The results were dramatic. A full month after this visit, the callers in group 3 showed average increases of 142 percent in weekly time spent on the phone. They raised 171 percent more money. Callers in groups 1 and 2, who did not meet the scholarship student, showed no changes in performance. A surprisingly strong effect for spending a few minutes talking with a scholarship student![4]

But is it surprising? It is if you don't know about seeking systems, and you approach the job of management with an industrial revolution lens. From that perspective, it's inefficient to waste time talking with the end user. And from that perspective, it's more efficient to improve the script and then create measures, incentives, and punishments so that employees know they are being watched.

Once you know about how the seeking system operates, however, you can make better predictions about triggering employees' enthusiasm and performance.

Teaming up with Dave Hoffmann, a professor at the University of North Carolina, Grant expanded his fundraiser research and gathered a new set of data from a whole new set of callers at another location. In this follow-up study, Grant and Hoffman again asked a scholarship recipient to explain to a group of fundraisers how the scholarship had affected his life in positive ways.[5]

Now, here is my favorite part of this study. Grant and Hoffman then compared the effects of this intervention to the same type of message delivered by a leader. In this condition, a different set of fundraisers heard an ideological message from their leader about the importance of the work that fundraisers perform, how even small donations can make a large difference, and how the donations are used to benefit other people in the university.

This second approach is usually how purpose is "done" in organizations—if it is done at all—that is, by leaders who see it as their job to communicate the *company's* purpose. But it didn't work very well in the fundraiser study. Results showed no significant improvements in how much money fundraisers brought in when the boss explained the organization's purpose.

However, the message from the student replicated Grant's first investigation. Fundraisers who received the student's gratitude raised a *lot* more money than those who didn't: an average of $9,704.58 versus $2,459.44—an almost 400 percent difference. Nothing else in the environment changed: the company didn't change the database, or invest in new phones, or paint the walls a funky color, or put a sliding board down to the break room.

The reason why the scholarship student had an outsize impact on the fundraisers is that he connected with them emotionally. And that's the thing about purpose: in order to activate the seeking system, it needs to be *felt*. Purpose is not something logical and rational, something you hear about and then process in a cognitive way. Grant and Hoffman's data suggested that fundraisers' seeking systems were activated when they felt the gratitude from the scholarship students, firsthand, but not when they heard the same message from their supervisor. Even though what the supervisor said to the fundraisers about the purpose of their work was rational and logical, it did not touch them emotionally or activate their seeking systems.

Simply telling someone the purpose of their work is like telling them about a good book that you have read. Even if it *is* good, they probably won't recommend it to one of their friends until they read it themselves and experience it firsthand.

That doesn't mean that leaders can't help instill purpose in others and encourage them to find greater meaning in their work.

They definitely can, if they invest in employees experiencing their impact on others firsthand. And as I have learned, leaders also need to align their approach with their own *personal* sense of purpose.

Here is a story that helps me explain (there's a twist ending).

Phishing for Purpose

Once, I was explaining Grant's fundraising study to a group of leaders from F. Hoffmann-La Roche AG, one of the world's largest pharmaceutical companies. As I told the Roche leaders about the results, one of them lit up and blurted out "This just happened to us! I just saw this happen last year!" I asked her to tell us what happened.

She explained how her team worked in the medical-devices division. Her group was sometimes looked down upon by people in the organization who thought that chemistry was "more sexy" than engineering. Many people in the division were not fully engaged, and the morale of the team was pretty low. One day the leader arranged for a customer to tell the team her personal story.

This customer had diabetes and had to test her blood daily to make sure her insulin dose was right. Unfortunately, this poor woman misunderstood how much blood was needed and was pricking her finger more than she needed to in order to get the blood. It not only hurt every day, so that it became something she dreaded, but she also was making a mess of her fingers. She would work her way down one finger from the tip to the knuckle, get it all inflamed and sometimes infected, before moving to the next finger. She said it got to the point where she would sit on her hand to hide the damage from others. She stopped going out to dinner because she was so embarrassed.

The diabetic then told the group how they had improved her life when they invented a little finger-pricking device. You put it on the end of your finger and click it. It takes the absolute minimum amount of blood, is almost painless and leaves almost no cut at all. She told how, because of this device, her hands have healed, and she can go out to dinner without feeling ashamed about herself. She told the group: "You people changed my life."

The Roche leader told us that the medical device team was really affected by this patient testimonial. She said that it was very emotional in the room during the meeting. And for months, people were more jazzed up and working harder and better. The team's creativity and enthusiasm were higher than she'd ever seen it.

As the professor listening to this account, I was happy the leader had shared this story. It added a lot of credibility to the power of purpose in activating the seeking system. This story also supported the findings from Grant's fundraiser research, because it showed the same effects occurred in a very different industry. As I was basking in satisfaction, another leader on the other side of the room raised his hand.

"Yeah, they tried that bullshit on us too," he said.

His cynical tone was not exactly what I wanted to hear, but it definitely sounded like we were going to get a different perspective. He continued: "I have this boss who has *never* talked about anything but quarterly profits and hitting shipping targets.

Well, he must have come to London Business School and heard you talk about this study because one day he drags a patient in to our weekly meeting and makes her tell us this story of how the drugs saved her life. I mean, trying to exploit our emotions to make us work harder? Using a *patient* to manipulate us!? That's pretty low."

I learned so much through this exchange. It not only matters *what* leaders do, it also matters *why they are doing it*. When it comes to increasing a sense of purpose, the same tactic of connecting employees with their customers can be viewed as inspirational or manipulative, depending on why the employees think the leader is doing it. This could even be why the leader's words didn't improve results in Grant's fundraiser study.

If a leader's purpose-building events are seen as authentic—consistent with what the leader really cares about—then the effect can be inspirational. People experience the purpose of their actions and feel their seeking systems kick in. However, if employees think that a leader has just learned a new trick to get more out of them, the identical event can backfire. Employees can feel manipulated, disgusted, and demotivated. This means that "purpose tactics" can fail badly when employees feel their emotions are being exploited by leaders who only care about their bonus. The Roche leader coined the phrase "phishing for purpose" for this phenomenon.

Even though this learning bowled me over at the time, in retrospect perhaps this isn't so surprising. If a leader tries to convince us that our work has some grand purpose that we don't believe in, and she or he has not personally acted consistent with that purpose in the past, we question the leader's motives. After all, our emotions have evolved over millions of years, and they are really smart. On average, our ancestors who were good at resisting deception and detecting sincerity in others were probably less likely to get tricked, and more likely to survive and have resources for their children.[6]

So it's pretty likely that we evolved into effective authenticity-detection machines: we are attracted to authenticity and repulsed by insincerity. Just as we have evolved to be disgusted by rotten meat because it will make us ill, we have evolved to be disgusted by insincere attempts to manipulate us.

It's not expensive to build purpose experiences into work, but it does take creativity and a leadership mindset in which leaders (a) understand why purpose is important to people, and (b) personally gain a sense of purpose when they help employees experience a sense of purpose.

In chapter 9, we are going to look at other techniques leaders have used to help employees develop their narratives about the purpose and meaning of their work. We will see how people's stories about their work behaviors can range from "how I do my work" to "why I do my work." Leaders' investments into personalizing purpose make the difference.

CHAPTER 9

CRAFTING NARRATIVES ABOUT PURPOSE

Rick Garrelfs, who was a leader at Rabobank for eighteen years, told me about an experience he developed to help high-potential employees understand the meaning of their work. Working with a consulting organization, Garrelfs and his team told the sixty employees: "At 5 a.m., be at Eindhoven [a city in the northern part of the Netherlands] Central station." They did not divulge any further information to the participants, which naturally caused some curiosity and concerns. Some of the people called and protested, "But the trains are not running at 5 a.m." or "I live far away, so I will need a hotel." To which the team responded by saying: "Yes, that is correct" to retain the curiosity.

People started arriving at the station from 4:30, and the team made sure the café was open and coffee and rolls were available.

Around 5:15, Garrelfs started walking from the station (the group followed naturally at that point) into a waiting coach, which took them on a thirty-minute drive into the dark, away from town. The bus stopped, the group exited and started walking into the fields, with Garrelfs in front with a light, and someone from the consulting firm with a light at the rear.

After thirty minutes, they arrived at a line of trees, where they saw a man standing with a candle. As the group gathered around him, still in the dark of early morning, the man started to speak about the situation of farmers in the late nineteenth century in the southern Netherlands. He spoke about the farmers' daily problems, their poverty, and the harshness of their existence. He described how the Dutch priest, Pater Gerlacus van den Elsen, used his local influence to bring farmers together, so that those that had some money could lend it to those that didn't for investment.

As the man spoke, the sun slowly started to light the scene—the landscape and the group of people—and the group recognized the speaker. He was Bert Mertens, the senior executive of Cooperative Affairs and Governance of Rabobank, direct report to the executive board. Mertens was seen as the "conscience" of cooperative thinking in the bank. His core message: Rabobank emerged from the misery of farmers, and we should never forget that. Mertens was a real believer in the concept of humble leadership described by Jungkiu at Standard Chartered Bank, which we saw back in chapter 7.[1]

Mertens then walked the group across the farm fields, to a house where they were served breakfast by the farmers, who were long-time members of Rabobank. The farmers talked about the life of farming now, the difficulty of keeping a medium-sized farm alive, and what they did to make ends meet.

Although this had only been the start of the first day of a program, years later the participants picked out this particular moment as perhaps the most important experience for them in terms of understanding the meaning of Rabobank.

It is one thing for a leader to talk in a meeting about the mission of connecting banking to agriculture. This can be logical and strategic, and a leader can even put pictures of farms on the PowerPoint deck. It is another thing to have a personal experience: to walk in the fields, to connect with nature in the early morning, to eat and talk with the farmers who you serve as a bank. Imagine how this firsthand experience could change employees' stories about why they do what they do, and how it might help newcomers fashion their own purpose story. This sense of purpose could help employees make decisions that align with Rabobank's purpose, but also help them see their work as something worth doing.

Purpose Is a Personal Interpretation

As we saw in the Roche example in chapter 8, activating employees' seeking systems with purpose can be complicated. Leaders can't hand out purpose like playing cards. They can't just write up the purpose in the annual report and expect to activate employees' seeking systems. Your feeling of purpose depends on the meaning that you yourself place on your activities: Why do *you* think you are doing the things you are doing?

For example, what do you think you are doing *right now*? We all have an answer to this question, even if it is not salient to us, and even if it is not top of mind. We all have a story running around in our brain about what we think we are doing, at all times.[2]

For example, all of us *could* honestly say, "I am moving my eyes." Because it is true if you are reading this. Your eyes are in fact moving. Most of us would not answer the question this way, focusing on how our physical body was behaving. But if you did answer the question this way, psychologists would call this a *low level of construal*. A low level of construal, or interpretation, emphasizes the *how* element of our behavior, in terms of how you are moving your physical self.[3] This answer would be the equivalent of the fundraisers saying, "I'm talking into the phone." It's physical and observable, just reporting what our body is doing. These types of responses don't assign much longer-term, higher-order interpretation about *why* we are doing what we are doing.

You could also answer, "I'm reading." If you answered with this story, it would shift the emphasis from your physical body into an activity with a purpose. Yes, you are moving your eyes across the page, but in the spirit of something bigger, which is reading a book (and, thank you for making it this far, by the way). The answer "I'm reading" would invoke not only your external, physical body. This story also would have some implications for your brain and why it is processing new input. It would bring cognitions and some sense of why into the picture. For the fundraisers, this might be the equivalent of saying "I'm trying to get people to donate money."

We read for different reasons, however. Some of us might have the story "I'm reading this homework because this book is assigned for a required class, and it is due tomorrow." This homework story is a higher level of construal. This story puts some emphasis on the brain, and definitely has a personal meaning or end state in mind. There is a *why* and not just a *how* in this story. For example, perhaps this is required reading in a required class, so your story would be "I am reading this to get my MBA."

Now, what happens if the real reason you want an MBA is to learn finance and how to value companies? If this were the case (and believe me, it often is!), understanding how purpose works may not mean much to you personally. If that is the case, then your story actually might be "I'm reading a required chapter on fluffy organizational behavior bullshit because it will be on the test." This story doesn't really require much of you—it won't lead you to change any of your real beliefs and behaviors. And your commitment to the activity would be lower, if that is the story. You might be willing to stop if a better option came up, such as your friends getting together in a local pub (and believe me, they often are!).

Someone else might be getting her MBA because she wants to improve the engagement and creativity of people in her company. She might be reading the same words as you, right now, but if you asked her what she was doing she might say, "I am learning how to help people be more alive at work."

Her answer, which focuses on learning, would imply that she is comparing the ideas she reads with the ideas that she already held in her brain, and then deciding whether she wants to update anything. This story implies a much more active process. It is open to challenging long-held assumptions, and it brings emotions like curiosity and excitement into the picture. And it's more than just learning: it is learning how to make a positive effect on others. This reader is reading in order to help others engage themselves at work.

The *why* is very strong in this story, and the *how* is not as important. This story, with its high level of construal, would prompt the reader's commitment to stick with the reading, and stay actively involved in the learning, even if the concepts became difficult and even if the pub option became available.

Choosing Our Stories

Here is the most important thing: each of these answers can be true. In terms of what you are doing as you read this book, for example, you personally get to decide. Just like telling ourselves "I'm excited" before a math test in order to interpret our physiological reactions, we get to generate the narrative of our actions: What do our actions mean to us? Why are we doing what we are doing?[4]

Take Candice Billups, for example. She has worked for over thirty years as a janitor at the Comprehensive Cancer Center at the University of Michigan.[5] On the one hand, Billups's daily tasks may not sound enviable: society often frames janitorial work as unskilled and even "dirty."[6] She could focus on the repetition of mopping the floors and refilling the soap dispensers.

However, Billups interprets her work in a different way. When asked to describe it, she replies, "I am basically there for the patients . . . my relationship with the families is really important to me . . . I see myself as a positive force at the Cancer Center."[7] Billups focuses on the *why* of the work in a way that is meaningful to her (helping patients through a difficult time) rather than her repetitive tasks. Of course, both are true—but we have considerable latitude to focus on one story or the other. And, since our behaviors follow our stories, Billups makes it a point to get to know patients and their families to understand their needs. She brings a positive attitude to help them to smile even in the difficult circumstances. She humanizes the hospital for the patients. She says: "I try and have a smile on my face every day, no matter what's going on at home or with the department with coworkers. When the patients see me, they have to see a smile. Because you have to understand that when they come here they are very sick. They don't want come to an environment where everybody is frowning and pouting, and there is a fighting amongst each other. So I try to always, always have a smile."

By reframing her work's purpose around something that is meaningful and personal to her, Billups brings a different level of energy to her tasks, and also expands her set of behaviors at work (e.g., taking on extra tasks like getting to know the patients).

Once, I needed to develop a story about chemotherapy. Every other week for six months, I needed to receive chemo for a lymphoma. For my first session, I told myself a poison story. And it's a fact—chemo is really toxic; for example, it can't even touch your skin because it will burn you. And I was letting a medical team inject that poison into my body. It was invasive, and I felt strong negative emotions: anxiety, fear, dread, and disgust. I fought back my panic as the chemo slid into my port. It seemed to make my chest cold and I tasted metal in my mouth.

Looking back, I can see my poison story made me feel that I had to fight the chemo. It was hard to get out of bed on chemo days when I told myself that story. I had to fight back a flight response as I walked into the Gravely Clinical Cancer Center on the University of North Carolina campus. I remember how hard it was to write and be creative in this emotional state. I had my computer with me, and there was no logical reason why I couldn't use the time to write. But it was hard to concentrate or make progress as the chemo session crawled by. By the end of the three hours, I felt emotionally brittle.

Lee Berkowitz, my doctor and hero, helped me craft a different story. He helped me see how lucky I was to have this medicine. Chemo was invented the year I was born, and doctors hadn't figured out how to treat Hodgkin's lymphoma successfully until about 1980. If I had been born ten years earlier, I would have just had to watch as the life drained out of me. With Berkowitz's story, a lot changed for me. Even though it was the same chemo, I focused on how the medicine was going to let me see my kids grow up. It still wasn't fun, of course, but I felt gratitude and hope.

Like Adam Grant's fundraisers and workers in Roche R&D lab (chapter 8), nothing changed in my actual environment. The same substance was going into my body in the same room. But, the new story changed the chemo session for me, from resisting it because it was hurting me, to accepting it because it was helping me. Because my emotions turned from negative to positive, my resilience and energy improved. I used the large chunk of time to make lots of progress on my book. The story that we generate and tell ourselves can have huge effects on our behaviors and the results that we create.[8]

In a related example, Steve Cole, the UCLA professor of medicine whom you read about in chapter 1, used the power of stories to create a video game that helps kids deal with chemotherapy.[9] In addition to his full-time work as a professor, Cole is Vice President for Research at HopeLab, an organization focused on enhancing the health and well-being of young people with chronic diseases. HopeLab built the video game "Re-Mission" where players pilot a nanobot through the bodies of teenaged cancer patients to destroy cancer cells, eradicate bacteria, and manage treatment side effects.[10] Cole told me: "The video game is sort of a 'rebranding of chemo' as a weapon in the fight against cancer. One of the goals of the game is to move 'chemo' in semantic space from being something primarily perceived as *part* of cancer (and alien to one's prior and aspired future identity as a normal healthy human) and toward something *on your side* as you fight a foe."

The results of several well-crafted studies show that playing the game, but not other video games, activates patients' mesolimbic neural circuits associated with intrinsic motivation.[11] You guessed it: by making the story of a video game personally meaningful and purposeful, Cole and his team activated kids' seeking systems. Sort of like the playing *World of Warcraft*, described back in chapter 1. As Cole told me, "We're just beginning to appreciate how much intrinsic motivation processes affect gene expression and cellular function."

Purpose, Pain, and Perseverance

When it comes to the stories we tell ourselves, the *why* of our behaviors is a more powerful story than the *how*. Both philosophy and empirical research suggest that the higher our level of interpretation or construal, the more we will stick with it when the going gets hard. For example, let's think about trying to lose fifteen pounds. Maybe your doctor has told you that the extra weight is unhealthy. How might making the tough, daily decisions to maintain a healthy diet depend on your story about why you eat?

Consider your choice between a healthy salad (with no dressing!) and a pizza for lunch after the fourth day (or the fourth hour!) on your diet. If you tell yourself a low-level construal story of why you eat, you would focus on how your *body* feels. This story would focus you on your physical sensation of a gnawing tummy and the unpleasant psychological sensation of being hungry. And then you look at the salad. It looks lame. As Wharton professor Katherine Milkman and her colleagues say, "A low-level construal of a salad would focus on its taste and its likelihood of leaving you hungry."[12] If your story of why you eat centers on your body, right now, and you are thinking about the salad's ability to fulfill your immediate physical prompts, you will likely get the pizza. And most diets end this way—unsuccessfully.

If, however, you tell yourself a high-level construal story of why you eat, you might focus on your health, and your long-term goals of losing fifteen pounds. With this story, why would you put something unhealthy in your body that would add weight and make your heart work too hard? Says Milkman, "A high-level construal of a salad would focus on the salad's healthfulness and its likelihood of increasing longevity."[13] The story you tell yourself about eating changes your behavior, and you are more likely to choose the salad. Twenty minutes later, when your snarling belly is appeased, you feel pride instead of guilt.

As Friedrich Nietzsche said, "He who has a why to live can bear with almost any how."[14]

When we personally understand and believe in the *why* of our actions, we have greater resilience and stamina when the going gets tough. We saw this clearly in the fundraisers' behaviors described in chapter 8. When they felt the gratitude of the students, they were reminded of the *why* of their work, and changed their story. As their story focused less on the what of their physical movements (making phone calls) and more on the why of those calls (helping students go to college), they became more likely to persevere through rejection from the people they called.

Exercise is another good example of how much construal matters when the going gets tough. It's an example that many of us can relate to as we start and stop our fitness regimes. Think about what happens when you run up a hill and you start to feel discomfort. This discomfort is produced by your heart rate as it goes up to 140 or 150. In fact, this is the *job* of heart rate: to get your attention when you are working hard and to ask you "are you sure about this? Are you sure you want this?" It is, of course, possible for us to interpret these uncomfortable signals as "pain."

But really it depends on what you think you are doing. If you are using a low level of construal, focusing on your physical body and how it feels right now, you might think of the act of exercise as "moving my legs." If this is how you see it, it makes sense to stop running and walk when going up the hill hurts. Why would you want to hurt? If there is no good answer in your story, then it's all pain with no gain. What's the point? Same thing if your day starts getting busy with meetings and other demands: it's painful to try and keep that forty-five minutes open for exercise and a shower. And so when the schedule gets tight, the exercise gets cut.

But what happens if your story about exercise is "to make my day better with endorphins"? Endorphins are morphine-like chemicals produced by the body during exercise that trigger positive feelings. If *this* was your story, you might lean a little farther into the same level of discomfort when your heart rate makes itself known. Because this story means that the discomfort has a point—it allows you to reinterpret the same signal from your heart rate differently. Yes there is discomfort, but in fact this is a signal that your exercise is *working*—this elevated heart rate releases endorphins and gives you positive feelings and a sense of accomplishment as you go through the rest of your day. The same heart-rate information, using this story, is a sign that you are making progress toward where you want to be.

The point here, of course, is not that you should change your story about why you eat or exercise (although endorphins are free, legal, good drugs that make life a better place to be). The broader point is to think about how the same behaviors and activities take on very different meaning to us depending on the stories we tell ourselves about what we are doing. If we choose more meaningful stories about our work based on personal experience and interpretations of our impact, we can light up our seeking systems and change our motivation, perseverance, and resilience in the face of adversity.

As leaders, if we find ways to invest in purpose experiences for employees, so that they can experience their impact firsthand, we can activate their seeking systems. Given the importance of authenticity around the purpose topic, the best thing you can do as a leader is use your creativity and courage to offer immersive experiences to employees so that they can witness the impact of their work on others. You can help them *experience* purpose rather than trying to *issue* purpose.

It is worth investing in personalized purpose because employees' emotions beat logic when it comes to changing their narratives about the meaning of their work. Logically and rationally, it would have made more sense for Nokian to just tell employees that ice tires are cool and then give the employees €1,000 to increase engagement. Production employees might even *say* that they would just prefer the money. But most employees would not have used the money to create an impactful life event that changed their core narrative about work and improved their sense of purpose about what they do all day.

The key for leaders is to make the purpose experiences thoughtful, creative, and meaningful. Let's look at some more examples.

Client Connections

Dr. James Goodnight, the CEO of SAS, the world's largest software services company, once told me about an initiative that has stuck with me ever since. The idea is simple. Software engineers go on-site with one of SAS's clients each year. So, for example, a software design person might spend a week at Bank of America with the point of contact there, helping the Bank of America person do his or her work and trying to understand what issues that person is facing and trying to solve.

The SAS programmer, in turn, gets a chance to see how the client is using—or not using—the features in the software. She might observe, for example, that the client was exporting data to an Excel spreadsheet to create a graph, when in fact the SAS software was programmed with that function. The client's behaviors would show the programmer that the graph function is too hard to find, or too clunky to use. This not only allows SAS's programmer to directly observe people using and working with this year's products, but gives them personal ideas about future fixes and new product ideas to design over the next year.

Think about this type of immersive client experience policy from two different lenses. First, use a logical, Industrial Revolution efficiency lens: this is a dumb policy that makes little sense at all. To give highly paid software engineers weeks off each year? Paying programmers to *not* do software programming? This could be viewed as a glorified vacation, and certainly most software firms do not have this policy in place.

Now take a seeking system perspective. The policy is genius. It gives people direct, firsthand experiences with the outcome of their work. It lets employees develop their own narrative about how they affect the lives of others. They get to see their impact, which activates their seeking systems and builds enthusiasm and intrinsic motivation to serve clients. Notice how the purpose experience does not change the actual work of programming, and it also does not somehow make programming into a humanitarian concern. SAS is still not curing diseases or putting kids through school. But employees' feelings of purpose increase dramatically, because they can directly witness their effect on other people. And the practice also ignites employees' seeking systems because it encourages them to invent, experiment, and try out their own ideas.

What is the cost of helping employees develop a sense of purpose? What is needed is not a lot of money, but a new story of what leaders think they should be doing as leaders. According to Goodnight: "Many executives are too obsessed with short-term numbers-based management. With their eyes only on the short term, they fail to recognize and cultivate long-term opportunities such as research and development, employee and customer longevity, and education for the next generation."[15]

Customizing Purpose

When I was in Vienna talking with a different senior leadership team from Roche, I was confused that the meeting took place at Microsoft's state-of-the-art offices. When I asked why Roche's high-level meeting was taking place at Microsoft, I learned that the two companies had built a close relationship over the last three years. How that relationship developed is similar to SAS's process described above.

Ten years ago, Microsoft made and sold standardized products. We've all used them. While there obviously were client account managers for these products, they really didn't need to know very much about the clients' needs. The software just worked. Dr. Dorothee Ritz, the Microsoft country manager, told me how Microsoft CEO Satya Nadella's digital transformation shook the company's assumptions about how to add value to the marketplace. To remain relevant, Microsoft was going to have to get good at customizing solutions for clients' particular needs and problems. For example, Microsoft needed to learn about Roche's business model in order to develop an intelligent product that addressed a dysfunctional piece of the supply chain.

In the past, Microsoft account managers would have talked to clients now and then. But under the new model, they needed to get out in the field, experience the clients' problems, and help devise solutions. So Ritz encouraged them to. One account manager spent a week out on the street with police officers, trying to understand when and where remote data could help them. Another account manager spent two days in a hospital to observe firsthand and understand what it would really mean to become paperless.

Ritz told me that these immersion experiences were enlightening for people. She said they came back illuminated, as in "lit up." They "got it" from a customer perspective. It was clear to her that the experiences increased their sense of purpose, since they witnessed the *why* of their work. Employees dove into their projects with more energy and enthusiasm after they had witnessed the clients' needs themselves.

So after a year of experimenting with this initiative, Ritz put something more secure in place. She selected a set of key customers (whom she calls *partners*) across industries ranging from car manufacturing to retailers to hospitals. And then fifteen people from Microsoft—teams ranging from senior leaders to associates—went on-site at each company and asked lots of people at lots of different levels: "What are your challenges?" They talked to people in IT, of course, but they also talked with business decision makers across different functions.

At Tesla, for example, Ritz told me how Microsoft employees at different levels got to practice a conversation that started with Tesla's needs instead of Microsoft's products. They focused on holes in the process that Tesla needed to address. The Microsoft team came away with a few new contacts, and they felt empowered to be part of future conversations. But, Ritz said, even more important, they understood the direction of the project based on witnessing the situation and hearing about Tesla's issues firsthand.

Ritz also found that lower-level Microsoft employees asked very different questions from managers and leaders, which increased the company's credibility with the customers. For example, at a major retailer, a Microsoft employee who was close to the Xbox asked some very grounded questions about issues with the console. This led to a useful, practical discussion rather than high-level executive speak, which helped move the whole conversation toward solutions that the team could go back and work on. Imagine the sense of impact that the employee felt.

Ritz also told me that when the Microsoft executives heard these questions and the multiple angles of intelligence from these employees, they said, "I should bring that person into my team meetings more often." Ritz told me, "We found that getting to know each other better in the context of solving a partner's problems was more meaningful and a far better team-building experience than ropes exercises or off-site discussions."

This process of taking teams of Microsoft employees into partner organizations resulted in them developing a stronger sense of purpose. And in the case of Roche, it also led to a trust-based collaboration resulting in three Microsoft employees, including Ritz, being part of Roche's high-level meeting.

The purpose experiences described above were successful for a number of reasons: They allowed employees to witness the impact of their jobs firsthand. They also encouraged employees to develop and try out new ideas, which made their work feel more meaningful. As a result, they were able to develop deeper and more personal narratives about why they do what they do.

This is the power of purpose: it activates the seeking system and makes life feel better, as we saw in the company stories recounted throughout this book (see figure 9-1). Employees are less likely to get sick, and they live longer. These benefits are, of course, on top of the fact that clients appreciate being listened to and helped with their business challenges.

When we understand the powerful humanistic results of purpose—not to mention the economic benefits of building purpose

FIGURE 9-1

Experiencing purpose activates the seeking system

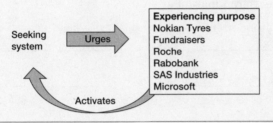

into businesses—then our quest as leaders changes. Our mission moves from "How can I make this job more efficient, predictable, and controlled?" to "How can I give my team firsthand experiences that allow them to personalize the meaning of their work?" This is a powerful new way to think about employment—as a chance to light up employees' seeking systems instead of shutting them down.

Legacy, Leadership, and Purpose

Let's try a last exercise. Write all four of your grandparents' names on the lines below:

My mother's mother: My father's mother:

_____   _____

My mother's father: My father's father:

_____   _____

Lots of people can list these four names, and lots of people can't. Nothing to be ashamed of. Now, write down all eight names of your great-grandparents:

_____   _____

_____   _____

_____   _____

_____   _____

Don't feel bad if you don't get them all, lots of people can't get even *one*.

And that's legacy for us: our own family isn't going to remember our names in two generations. Let's take a different example. Penicillin is one of human's greatest inventions. Do you know who invented penicillin? Do you know who invented electrical resistors? You get the point.

Lots of leaders spend time thinking about their legacy, but really all we have are the positive effects that we can have on each other today. As leaders, we have a chance to make life more meaningful, and more worth living, for the people we lead. This will help our companies stay relevant and agile, but the stakes are much higher than that.

In chapter 8, we saw how a Roche employee was disgusted when he didn't believe his leader's attempts to highlight purpose were authentic. It's hard to inspire others when you are not feeling inspired. To be effective, you need a purpose for leading that you really believe in. Perhaps that purpose could be to make people feel more alive at work: to make life more worth living for the employees you serve.

It seems to me that nobody talks about it, but leaders have duties that are similar to religious figures. This is because they have such a direct effect on the purpose that people feel about their work and feel in their lives. And in this sense, leaders serve as doctors too. Because we now know that employees' sense of purpose directly affects their health and longevity.

When we accept the role of helping others find meaning in the place where they spend most of their waking hours and we improve their health, it will give us more meaning and health in our *own* lives.

Or at least that could be the story we tell ourselves.

Do you believe it?

NOTES

Introduction: Our Organizations Are Letting Us Down

1. A. Adkins, "Majority of U.S. Employees Not Engaged Despite Gains in 2014," Gallup, January 28, 2015; S. Adams, "Unhappy Employees Outnumber Happy Ones by Two to One Worldwide," *Forbes*, October 10, 2013; M. Buckingham, D. O. Clifton, *Now, Discover Your Strengths* (New York: The Free Press, 2004).

2. J. Hagel et al., "Passion at Work," Deloitte Insights, October 7, 2014, https://dupress.deloitte.com/dup-us-en/topics/talent/worker-passion-employee-behavior.html.

3. J. Panksepp, *Affective Neuroscience: The Foundations of Human and Animal Emotions* (Oxford: Oxford University Press, 2005).

4. J. M. Dutcher et al., "Self-Affirmation Activates the Ventral Striatum: A Possible Reward-Related Mechanism for Self-Affirmation," *Psychological Science* 27, no. 4 (2016): 1–12.

5. M. J. Koepp et al., "Evidence for Striatal Dopamine Release During a Videogame," *Nature* 393 (1998): 266–268.

6. K. C. Berridge and T. E. Robinson, "What Is the Role of Dopamine in Reward: Hedonic Impact, Reward Learning, or Incentive Salience?" *Brain Research Reviews* 28 (1998): 309–369; T. Randin, *Animals Make Us Human: Creating the Best Life for Animals* (New York: Houghton Mifflin Harcourt, 2009).

7. C. Izard, "Basic Emotions, Natural Kinds, Emotion Schemas, and a New Paradigm," *Perspectives in Psychological Science* 2, no. 3 (September 2007): 260–280.

8. R. M. Nesse, "Fear and Fitness: An Evolutionary Analysis of Anxiety Disorders," *Ethology and Sociobiology* 15, no. 5 (1994): 247–261; B. Fredrickson, *Positivity* (New York: Random House, 2009).

9. M. E. P. Seligman et al., "Positive Psychology Progress: Empirical Validation of Interventions," *American Psychologist* 60 (2005): 410–421.

10. T. D. Wilson, *Strangers to Ourselves: Discovering the Adaptive Unconscious* (Cambridge, MA: Belknap Press of Harvard University Press, 2002).

11. Panksepp, *Affective Neuroscience*.

12. M. Fox, "Why Women Driven by Passion and Purpose Get Seats in Corporate Boardrooms," *Forbes*, December 22, 2016.

Chapter 1: The Way Things Ought to Be

1. B. A. Nardi, *My Life as a Night Elf Priest: An Anthropological Account of* World of Warcraft (Ann Arbor, MI: University of Michigan Press, 2010).

2. J. S. Brown and D. Thomas, "You Play *World of Warcraft?* You're Hired!" *Wired*, April 1, 2006, http://www.wired.com/2006/04/learn/.

3. N. Doshi and L. McGregor, *Primed to Perform: How to Build the Highest Performing Cultures Through the Science of Total Motivation* (New York: Harper Collins, 2015).

4. L. F. Barrett et al., "Of Mice and Men: Natural Kinds of Emotion in the Mammalian Brain?" *Perspectives on Psychological Science* 3, no. 2 (September 2007): 297–312.

5. C. Izard, "Basic Emotions, Natural Kinds, Emotion Schemas, and a New Paradigm," *Perspectives in Psychological Science* 2, no. 3 (September 2007): 260–280.

6. J. Panksepp, *Affective Neuroscience: The Foundations of Human and Animal Emotions* (Oxford: Oxford University Press, 2005), 144.

7. S. Blakeslee, "Running Late? Researchers Blame Aging Brain," *New York Times*, March 24, 1998, ww.nytimes.com/1998/03/24/science/running-late-researchers-blame-aging-brain.html?pagewanted=all.

8. Panksepp, *Affective Neuroscience*, 149.

9. C. Peterson et al., "Zest and Work," *Journal of Organizational Behavior* 30 (2009): 161–172; N. Park, C. Peterson, and M. E. P. Seligman, "Strengths of Character and Well-Being," *Journal of Social and Clinical Psychology* 23 (2004): 603–619.

10. A. W. Brooks, "Get Excited: Reappraising Pre-Performance Anxiety as Excitement," *Journal of Experimental Psychology: General* 143, no. 3 (2014): 1144–1158.

11. J. P. Jamieson et al., "Turning the Knots in Your Stomach into Bows: Reappraising Arousal Improves Performance on the GRE," *Journal of Experimental Social Psychology* 46 (2010): 208–212.

12. G. Ramirez and S. L. Beilock, "Writing about Testing Worries Boosts Exam Performance in the Classroom," *Science* 331 (2011): 211–213.

13. B. L. Fredrickson, "Positive Emotions Broaden and Build," in *Advances in Experimental Social Psychology*, vol. 47, ed. Patricia Devine and Ashby Plant (Burlington, MA: Academic Press, 2013), 1–53.

14. T. M. Jones, "Ethical Decision Making by Individuals in Organizations: An Issue-Contingent Model," *Academy of Management Review* 16, no. 2 (1991): 66–395.

15. J. Mendelson, "Ecological Modulation of Brain Stimulation Effects," *International Journal of Psychology* 2 (1972): 285–304.

16. J. S. Wright and J. Panksepp, "An Evolutionary Framework to Understand Foraging, Wanting, and Desire: The Neuropsychology of the SEEKING System," *Neuropsychoanalysis* 14, no. 1 (2012): 5–75.

17. Wright and Panksepp, "An Evolutionary Framework."

18. K. C. Berridge, T. E. Robinson, and J. W. Aldridge, "Dissecting Components of Reward: 'Liking,' 'Wanting,' and Learning," *Current Opinions in Pharmacology* 9 (2009): 65–73; E. Yoffe, "Seeking," *Slate*, August 12, 2009, http://www.slate.com/articles/health_and_science/science/2009/08/seeking.html; K. C. Berridge and T. E. Robinson, "What Is the Role of Dopamine in Reward: Hedonic Impact, Reward Learning, or Incentive Salience?" *Brain Research Reviews* 28 (1998): 309–369.

19. Yoffe, "Seeking."

20. A. H. Maslow, "A Theory of Human Motivation," *Psychological Review* 50 (1943): 370–396.

21. Wright and Panksepp, "An Evolutionary Framework."

22. R. Kraut, "Two Conceptions of Happiness," *Philosophical Review* 87 (1979): 167–196.

23. B. L. Fredrickson et al., "Psychological Well-Being and the Human Conserved Transcriptional Response to Adversity," *PLoS ONE* 10, no. 3 (2015): e0121839. doi:10.1371/journal.pone.0121839.

24. R. T. Howell, M. L. Kern, and S. Lyubomirsky, "Health Benefits: Meta-Analytically Determining the Impact of Well-Being on Objective Health Outcomes," *Health Psychology Review* 1 (2007): 83–136.

25. B. L. Fredrickson et al., "A Functional Genomic Perspective on Human Well-Being," *Proceedings of the National Academy of Sciences*

110, no. 33 (2013), www.pnas.org/cgi/doi/10.1073/pnas.1305419110; Fredrickson et al., "Psychological Well-Being"; S. W. Cole, "Human Social Genomics," *PLOS Genetics* 10 (2014), e1004601; S. Kitayama et al., "Cultural Sources of Personal Well-Being: Work, Meaning, and Gene Regulation," *Psychoneuroendocrinology* (2016).

26. E. E. Smith, "Meaning Is Healthier Than Happiness," *The Atlantic*, August 1, 2013, http://www.theatlantic.com/health/archive/2013/08/meaning-is-healthier-than-happiness/278250/.

27. Baumeister et al., "Some Key Differences between a Happy Life and a Meaningful Life," *Journal of Positive Psychology* 8, no. 6 (2013): 505–516; Smith, "Meaning Is Healthier Than Happiness."

28. Aristotle, *Nicomachean Ethics*, trans. T. Irwin (Indianapolis, IN: Hackett Publishing, 1985), 7.

29. D. Brown, *Happy: Why More or Less Everything Is Absolutely Fine* (London: Penguin, 1964), 52.

Chapter 2: The Way Things Are—and How to Make Them Better

1. M. E. P. Seligman, "Learned Helplessness," *Annual Review of Medicine* 23 (1972): 407–412.

2. M. Konnikova, "Inspiring Torture," *New Yorker*, January 14, 2015.

3. L. Y. Abramson, M. E. P. Seligman, and J. D. Teasdale, "Learned Helplessness in Humans: Critique and Reformulation," *Journal of Abnormal Psychology* 87 (1978): 49–74.

4. "Model T," History.com, http://www.history.com/topics/model-t.

5. F. Taylor, *The Principles of Scientific Management* (New York: Harper & Brothers, 1910).

6. *Oxford Living Dictionaries*, s.v. "Management," https://en.oxforddictionaries.com/definition/management.

7. S. C. Motta et al., "Dissecting the Brain's Fear System Reveals the Hypothalamus Is Critical for Responding in Subordinate Conspecific Intruders," *Proceedings of the National Academy of Sciences* 106 (2008): 4870–4875. doi: 10.1073/pnas.0900939106.

8. D. Kahneman, *Thinking, Fast and Slow* (London: Penguin, 2012); G. de Becker, *The Gift of Fear: Survival Signals That Protect Us from Violence* (New York: Random House, 2000).

9. J. S. Wright and J. Panksepp, "An Evolutionary Framework to Understand Foraging, Wanting, and Desire: The Neuropsychology of the SEEKING System," *Neuropsychoanalysis* 14, no. 1 (2012): 5–75.

10. J. Panksepp, *Affective Neuroscience: The Foundations of Human and Animal Emotions* (Oxford: Oxford University Press, 2005).

11. Malcolm Gladwell discusses this in "Blame Game," *Revisionist History* (podcast), episode 8, http://revisionisthistory.com/episodes/08-blame-game.

12. R. F. Baumeister, "Bad Is Stronger Than Good," *Review of General Psychology* 5 (2001): 323–370; B. Fredrickson, *Positivity* (New York: Random House, 2009).

13. "Reaching 50 Million Users," infographic, Visually, https://visual.ly/community/infographic/technology/reaching-50-million-users.

14. B. Goncalves, N. Perra, and A. Vespignani, "Validation of Dunbar's Number in Twitter Conversations," *PLoS ONE* 6, no. 8 (2011): e22656. 10.1371/journal.pone.0022656.

15. Y. N. Harari, *Sapiens: A Brief History of Humankind* (London: Random House, 2014).

16. Ibid.

17. J. G. March, "Exploration and Exploitation in Organizational Learning," *Organization Science* 2 (1991): 71–87.

18. Ibid.

19. A. Enayati, "Is There a Bias against Creativity?" *CNN*, March 28, 2012, http://www.cnn.com/2012/03/28/health/enayati-uncertainty/index.html.

20. B. M. Staw, "Why No One Really Wants Creativity," in *Creative Action in Organizations: Ivory Tower Visions and Real World Voices*, ed. C. Ford and D. A. Gioia (Thousand Oaks, CA: Sage Publications, 1995).

21. B. A. Hennessey and T. M. Amabile, "Creativity," *Annual Review of Psychology* 61 (2010): 569–598.

22. C. Nemeth, "Differential Contributions of Majority and Minority Influence," *Psychological Review* 93, no. 1 (1986): 23–32.

23. J. S. Mueller, S. Melwani, J. A. Goncalo, "The Bias Against Creativity: Why People Desire but Reject Creative Ideas," *Psychological Science* 3, no. 1 (2012).

24. M. Kilduff, "Deconstructing Organizations," *Academy of Management Review* 18 (1993): 13–31.

25. J. Goddard, "The Firm of the Future," *Business Strategy Review*, November 2016.

26. D. H. Pink, *Drive: The Surprising Truth About What Motivates Us* (Edinburgh: Canongate, 2010).

27. Valve, "Handbook for New Employees," http://www.valvesoftware.com/company/Valve_Handbook_LowRes.pdf.

28. C. Dijkmansa, P. Kerkhof, C. J. Beukeboom, "A Stage to Engage: Social Media Use and Corporate Reputation," *Tourism Management* 47 (2015): 58–67.

29. J. Mann, "KLM Shows How to Use Social Media During Ash Crisis, and Air France How Not To," Gartner Blog Network, April 18, 2010, https://blogs.gartner.com/jeffrey_mann/2010/04/18/klm-shows-how-to-use-social-media-during-ash-crisis-and-air-france-how-not-to/.

30. "KLM Sorry for Mexico Tweet after Dutch World Cup Win," BBC Newsbeat, June 30, 2014, http://www.bbc.co.uk/newsbeat/article/28086231/klm-sorry-for-mexico-tweet-after-dutch-world-cup-win.

31. Ibid.

32. A. Peveto, "KLM Surprise: How a Little Research Earned 1,000,000 Impressions on Twitter," *Digett*, January 11, 2011, http://www.digett.com/2011/01/11/klm-surprise-how-little-research-earned-1000000-impressions-twitter#sthash.PFy4OPNp.dpuf.

33. "KLM: Surprise," YouTube video, posted by thecreativecriminals on Februay 7, 2011, http://www.youtube.com/watch?v=Sh-JRoY7_LU.

34. J. Koetsier, "KLM's 150 Social Media Customer Service Agents Generate $25M in Annual Revenue," *VentureBeat*, May 21, 2015, http://venturebeat.com/2015/05/21/klms-150-social-media-customer-service-agents-generate-25m-in-annual-revenue/.

35. KLM, "KLM Wins Six Webby Awards," press release, April 26, 2017, http://news.klm.com/klm-wins-six-webby-awards/.

Chapter 3: Encouraging People to Bring Their Best Selves to Work

1. D. H. Gruenfeld et al., "Group Composition and Decision Making: How Member Familiarity and Information Distribution Affect Process and Performance," *Organizational Behavior and Human Decision Processes* 67 (1996): 1–15.

2. D. M. Cable and C. Parsons, "Socialization Tactics and Person-Organization Fit," *Personnel Psychology* 54 (2001): 1–22.

3. D. M. Cable, F. Gino, and B. Staats, "Breaking Them In or Eliciting Their Best? Reframing Socialization around Newcomers' Authentic Self-Expression," *Administrative Science Quarterly* 58 (2013): 1–36.

4. D. S. Yeager et al., "Breaking the Cycle of Mistrust: Wise Interventions to Provide Critical Feedback across the Racial Divide," *Journal of Experimental Psychology: General* 143, no. 2 (2014): 804–824. doi: 10.1037/a0033906.

5. L. M. Roberts et al., "Composing the Reflected Best-Self Portrait: Building Pathways for Becoming Extraordinary in Work Organizations," *Academy of Management Review* 30 (2005): 712–736.

6. D. L. Norton, *Personal Destinies: A Philosophy of Ethical Individualism* (Princeton, NJ: Princeton University Press, 1976).

7. B. L. Fredrickson, "Positive Emotions Broaden and Build," *Advances in Experimental Social Psychology* 47 (2013): 1–53.

8. F. G. Ashby and A. M. Isen, "A Neuropsychological Theory of Positive Affect and Its Influence on Cognition," *Psychological Review* 106 (1999): 529–550; J. D. Creswell et al., "Affirmation of Personal Values Buffers Neuroendocrine and Psychological Stress Responses." *Psychological Science* 16 (2005): 846–851.

9. Ibid.

10. J. M. Dutcher et al., "Self-Affirmation Activates the Ventral Striatum: A Possible Reward-Related Mechanism for Self-Affirmation," *Psychological Science* 27, no. 4 (2016): 1–12.

11. Roberts et al., "Composing the Reflected Best-Self Portrait."

12. P. F. Drucker, "Managing Oneself," *Harvard Business Review*, January 2005.

13. J. J. Lee, "Essays in Organizational Behavior" (PhD diss., Harvard University, 2017).

14. D. H. Gruenfeld et al., "Group Composition and Decision Making: How Member Familiarity and Information Distribution Affect Process and Performance," *Organizational Behavior and Human Decision Processes* 67 (1996): 1–15.

15. G. M. Wittenbaum, A. P. Hubbell, and C. Zuckerman, "Mutual Enhancement: Toward an Understanding of the Collective Preference for Shared Information," *Journal of Personality and Social Psychology* 77 (1999): 967–978; and S. Chaiken and C. Stangor, "Attitudes and Attitude Change," *Annual Review of Psychology* 38 (1987): 575–630.

16. Provided by essentic.com.

17. D. Whyte, *Crossing the Unknown Sea: Work as a Pilgrimage of Identity* (New York: Riverhead Books, 2001).

18. C. Harzer and W. Ruch, "When the Job Is a Calling: The Role of Applying One's Signature Strengths at Work," *Journal of Positive Psychology* 7 (2012): 362–371; A. S. Waterman, "Two Conceptions of Happiness: Contrasts of Personal Expressiveness (Eudaimonia) and Hedonic Enjoyment," *Journal of Personality and Social Psychology* (1993): 64, 678–691.

19. M. E. P. Seligman et al., "Positive Psychology Progress: Empirical Validation of Interventions," *American Psychologist* 60 (2005): 410–421.

20. Norton, *Personal Destinies.*

21. Whyte, *Crossing the Unknown Sea.*

Chapter 4: Promoting Self-Expression

1. A. Grant, J. Berg, and D. M. Cable, "Job Titles as Identity Badges: How Self-Reflective Titles Can Reduce Emotional Exhaustion," *Academy of Management Journal* 57 (2014): 1201–1225.

2. D. M. Cable, "Creative Job Titles Can Energize Workers," *Harvard Business Review*, May 2016, 24–25.

3. A. Edmondson, "Psychological Safety and Learning Behavior in Work Teams," *Administrative Science Quarterly* 44 (1999): 350–383.

4. R. S. Lazarus and S. Folkman, *Stress, Appraisal, and Coping* (New York: Springer, 1984).

5. T. Wujec, "Build a Tower, Build a Team," TED Talks, February 2010, https://www.ted.com/talks/tom_wujec_build_a_tower?language=en.

6. G. E. Kreiner, E. C. Hollensbe, and M. L. Sheep, "Where Is the 'Me' among the 'We'? Identity Work and the Search for Optimal Balance," *Academy of Management Journal* 49 (2006): 1031–1057.

7. M. B. Brewer, "Motivations Underlying Ingroup Identification: Optimal Distinctiveness and Beyond," in *Intergroup Relations: The Role of Motivation and Emotion*, ed. S. Otten, K. Sassenberg, and T. Kessler (New York: Psychology Press 2009), 3–22.

8. S. Taggar, "Individual Creativity and Group Ability to Utilize Individual Creative Resources: A Multilevel Model," *Academy of Management Journal* 45 (2002): 315–330.

9. R. J. Ely and D. A. Thomas, "Cultural Diversity at Work: The Effects of Diversity Perspectives on Work Group Processes and Outcomes," *Administrative Science Quarterly* 26 (2001): 229–273.

10. J. T. Polzer, L. P. Milton, and W. B. Swann, "Capitalizing on Diversity: Interpersonal Congruence in Small Work Groups," *Administrative Science Quarterly* 47 (2002): 296–324.

11. B. Rigoni and J. Asplund, "Developing Employees' Strengths Boosts Sales, Profit, and Engagement," *Harvard Business Review*, September 2016.

12. C. Guignon, *On Being Authentic* (New York: Routledge, 2004).

13. M. Weber, *The Protestant Ethic and the Spirit of Capitalism* (New York: Scribner, 1952).

14. J. M. Twenge, *Generation Me: Why Today's Young Americans Are More Confident, Assertive, Entitled—and More Miserable Than Ever Before* (New York: Free Press, 2006).

15. G. Petriglieri, J. L. Petriglieri, and J. D. Wood, "Fast Tracks and Inner Journeys: Crafting Portable Selves for Contemporary Careers," *Administrative Science Quarterly* (forthcoming 2017).

Chapter 5: Encouraging Serious Play

1. J. S. Wright and J. Panksepp, "An Evolutionary Framework to Understand Foraging, Wanting, and Desire: The Neuropsychology of the SEEKING System," *Neuropsychoanalysis* 14, no. 1 (2012): 5–75; J. Panksepp, et al., "Affective Neuroscience Strategies for Understanding and Treating Depression: From Preclinical Models to Three Novel Therapeutics," *Clinical Psychological Science* 2 (2014): 472–494.

2. J. Burgdorf, J. Panksepp, and J. R. Moskal, "Frequency-Modulated 50 kHz Ultrasonic Vocalizations: A Tool for Uncovering the Molecular Substrates of Positive Affect," *Neuroscience and Biobehavioral Reviews* 35 (2011): 1831–1836.

3. H. P. Madrid et al., "The Role of Weekly High-Activated Positive Mood, Context, and Personality in Innovative Work Behavior: A Multilevel and Interactional Model," *Journal of Organizational Behavior* 35, no. 2 (2014): 234–256.

4. A. C. Edmondson, "Framing for Learning: Lessons in Successful Technology Implementation," *California Management Review* 45 (2003): 34–54.

5. Edmondson, "Framing for Learning"; C. S. Dweck and E. I. Leggett, "A Social-Cognitive Approach to Motivation and Personality," *Psychological Review* 95, no. 2 (1988): 256–273.

6. J. M. Worley and T. L. Doolen, "The Role of Communication and Management Support in a Lean Manufacturing Implementation," *Management Decision* 44, no. 2 (2006): 228–245.

7. E. Abrahamson, "Avoiding Repetitive Change Syndrome," *Sloan Management Review* 45, no. 2 (2004): 93–95.

8. V. H. Denenberg, D. S. Kim, and R. D. Palmiter, "The Role of Dopamine in Learning, Memory, and Performance of a Water Escape Task," *Behavioural Brain Research* 148 (2004): 73–78.

Chapter 6: Expanding on Freedom and Creativity

1. T. M. Amabile, *Creativity in Context* (Boulder, CO: Westview Press, 1996).

2. D. Vandewalle et al., "The Influence of Goal Orientation and Self-Regulation Tactics on Sales Performance: A Longitudinal Field Test," *Journal of Applied Psychology* 84 (1994): 249–259.

3. R. Kanfer and P. L. Ackerman, "Motivation and Cognitive Abilities: An Integrative/Aptitude-Treatment Interaction Approach to Skill Acquisition," *Journal of Applied Psychology* 74 (1989): 657–690.

4. M. Arndt, "3M's Seven Pillars of Innovation," *BusinessWeek*, May 10, 2006; D. H. Pink, *Drive: The Surprising Truth About What Motivates Us* (Edinburgh: Canongate, 2010).

5. A. Campbell et al., "The Future of Corporate Venturing," *MIT Sloan Management Review* (2003).

6. "Shell—GameChanger," Strategos, http://www.strategos.com/client/shell-gamechanger/.

7. Ibid.

8. Jillian D'Onfro, "The Truth about Google's Famous '20% Time' Policy," *Business Insider*, April 2015, http://uk.businessinsider.com/google-20-percent-time-policy-2015-4.

9. A. Ross, "Why Did Google Abandon 20% Time for Innovation?" HR Zone, June 3, 2015, http://www.hrzone.com/lead/culture/why-did-google-abandon-20-time-for-innovation.

10. A. Truong, "Why Google Axed Its '20% Time' Policy," *Fast Company*, August 16, 2013, https://www.fastcompany.com/3015877/why-google-axed-its-20-policy.

11. D. Sivers, "How to Start a Movement," TED2010, February 10, 2010, http://www.ted.com/talks/derek_sivers_how_to_start_a_movement.html.

12. "More Wood Behind Fewer Arrows," Google Blog, July 20, 2011, https://googleblog.blogspot.co.uk/2011/07/more-wood-behind-fewer-arrows.html.

Chapter 7: Humble Leadership and Employees' Seeking Systems

1. B. P. Owens and D. R. Hekman, "Modeling How to Grow: An Inductive Examination of Humble Leader Behaviors, Contingencies, and Outcomes," *Academy of Management Journal* 55 (2012): 787–818.

2. M. E. Inesi, D. H. Gruenfeld, and A. D. Galinsky, "How Power Corrupts Relationships: Cynical Attributions for Others' Generous Acts," *Journal of Experimental Social Psychology* 48 (2012): 795–803.

3. Owens and Hekman, "Modeling How to Grow."

4. J. C. Magee and A. D. Galinsky, "Social Hierarchy: The Self-Reinforcing Nature of Power and Status," *Academy of Management Annals* 2 (2008): 1351–1398.

5. B. P. Owens and D. R. Hekman, "How Does Leader Humility Influence Team Performance? Exploring the Mechanisms of Contagion and Collective Promotion Focus," *Academy of Management Journal* 59 (2016): 1088–1111; R. C. Liden, "Servant Leadership and Serving Culture: Influence on Individual and Unit Performance," *Academy of Management Journal* 57 (2014): 1434–1452.

6. R. K. Greenleaf, *Servant Leadership: A Journey into the Nature of Legitimate Power and Greatness* (Mahwah, NJ: Paulist Press, 1977).

7. Owens and Hekman, "Modeling How to Grow."

8. D. D. Whitney and A. Trosten-Bloom, *The Power of Appreciative Inquiry: A Practical Guide to Positive Change* (San Francisco: Berrett-Koehler Publishers, 2010).

9. D. Kahneman, *Thinking, Fast and Slow* (London: Penguin, 2012).

Chapter 8: Helping Employees Experience the Impact of Their Work

1. For an impression of the factory: https://youtu.be/oUHEsk3KzVo.

2. You can find a video of his performance here: https://www.nokiantires.com/innovation/research-and-development/fastest-on-ice/fastest-on-ice-2011/.

3. P. L. Hill and N. A. Turiano, "Purpose in Life as a Predictor of Mortality across Adulthood," *Psychological Science* 25, no. 7 (2014): 1482–1486. doi: 10.1177/0956797614531799.

4. A. M. Grant, "The Significance of Task Significance: Job Performance Effects, Relational Mechanisms, and Boundary Conditions," *Journal of Applied Psychology* 93 (2008): 108–124.

5. A. M. Grant and D. A. Hofmann, "Outsourcing Inspiration: The Performance Effects of Ideological Messages from Leaders and Beneficiaries," *Organizational Behavior and Human Decision Processes* 116 (2011): 173–187; A. M. Grant, "How Customers Can Rally Your Troops," *Harvard Business Review*, June 2011.

6. C. F. Bond, Jr., K. N. Kahler, and L. M. Paolicelli, "The Miscommunication of Deception: An Adaptive Perspective," *Journal of Experimental Social Psychology* 21, no. 4 (1985): 21 331–345.

Chapter 9: Crafting Narratives about Purpose

1. R. K. Greenleaf, *Servant Leadership: A Journey into the Nature of Legitimate Power and Greatness* (Mahwah, NJ: Paulist Press, 1977).

2. R. R. Vallacher and D. A. Wegner, "What Do People Think They're Doing? Action Identification and Human Behavior," *Psychological Review* 94 (1987): 3–15.

3. K. Fujita et al., "Construal Levels and Self-Control," *Journal of Personality and Social Psychology* 90 (2006): 351–367.

4. T. Wilson, *Redirect: Changing the Stories We Live By* (London: Penguin, 2013).

5. You can watch Candice describing her work here: https://www.youtube.com/watch?v=r6JtlhhdjBw&feature=youtu.be.

6. B. E. Ashforth and G. E. Kreiner, "'How Can You Do It?': Dirty Work and the Challenge of Constructing a Positive Identity," *Academy of Management Review* 24 (1999): 413–434.

7. G. Spreitzer et al., "Toward Human Sustainability: How to Enable More Thriving at Work," *Organizational Dynamics* 41 (2012): 155–162.

8. Wilson, *Redirect*.

9. S. W. Cole, D. J. Yoo, and B. Knutson, "Interactivity and Reward-Related Neural Activation During a Serious Videogame," *PLoS ONE* 7, no. 3 (2012): e33909. doi:10.1371/journal.pone.0033909.

10. Learn more about the game at www.re-mission.net.

11. Cole, Yoo, and Knutson, "Interactivity and Reward-Related Neural Activation."

12. K. L. Milkman, T. Rogers, and M. H. Bazerman, "Harnessing Our Inner Angels and Demons: What We Have Learned About Want/Should Conflicts and How That Knowledge Can Help Us Reduce Short-Sighted Decision Making," *Perspectives on Psychological Science* 3 (2008): 324–338.

13. Ibid.

14. V. E. Frankl, *Man's Search for Meaning* (New York: Beacon Press, 2006), 76.

15. T. Bisoux, "Corporate Counter Culture," *BizEd* 4 (2004): 16–20.

INDEX

adrenaline, 33
alive feeling. *See* feeling alive
anxiety
    chemotherapy triggering,
      159–160
    employee learning affected by,
      87–88
    new employee's experience of,
      53, 56, 58–59
    new team members' experience
      of, 64
    performance situations trigger-
      ing, 19, 20, 90, 99–100, 128, 144
    relational best-self activation
      and, 63
    shutting off seeking systems and,
      31, 41
Aristotle, 26
Asplund, Jim, 76–77
Atlassian, 101
authority, and leadership, 118, 128

bank branch visits example of
    leadership, 115–123, 124, 126,
    135–136
Berg, Justin, 67–68, 69, 72

Berkowitz, Lee, 160
Berridge, Kent, 23
best selves stories, 53–66
    benefits of using, 59–60
    best selves concept definition
      in, 59
    errors in data entry tasks and, 61
    experiment comparing onboard-
      ing approaches with, 57–58
    feeling like ourselves at work
      and, 59–60, 61
    learning about ourselves from
      other's stories about us, 61–63
    need to activate, 60
    seeking system activation by, 61,
      65–66
    teams and, 64–65
    Wipro's individualized approach
      to, 53–56, 57, 58
    as wise intervention, 58–59
Billups, Candice, 158–159
Birkinshaw, Julian, 111–112
bonuses, 21, 99–100, 144, 150
brain
    awareness of current physical
      body activity and learning in,
      156–158

brain (*continued*)
    creativity link to negativity in, 43
    emotional systems and, 16–17
    fear system in, 33
    impulses to explore, experiment, and find new meaning based in, 24, 26, 33, 34
    innovation and change and systems in, 135
    learning environment producing dopamine in, 91
    online games' engagement of, 13–14
    seeking system's location in, 17, 23, 24, 26, 135
    wanting and liking systems in, 23
Brewer, Marilyn, 75
Brin, Sergey, 112
Brooks, Alison Wood, 19, 20–21
Brown, Derren, 27
bureaucratic leadership, 32, 124

change
    as chance to experiment and learn, 89–90
    emotional aspects of, 134
    employees' resistance to, 89
    humans' biological wiring for, 134–135
    need for new way of working and, 8–9, 36–37, 43
    wise interventions and pace of, 132
character strengths inventory, 66
Choi, Jungkiu, 116–123, 124, 126, 134
coaching programs, 77, 110–111, 130–131

cognitive abilities
    learned helplessness and, 30
    seeking system's urging of, 17, 20
Cole, Steve, 22–23, 26, 161
collaboration, 73, 74, 90, 129–130
commitment to work
    experimentation and, 95–96, 121
    narratives supporting, 157
    polls on lack of, 4
communication
    bank branch visits and, 122
    coaching programs for, 110–111
    food delivery service example of weekly meetings for, 130–134
    huddles with employees used for, 117, 118–119, 120
    KLM employees' use of social media for, 46–49
    by leaders of company's purpose, 146–147
    teams and, 64, 75, 90
    World of Warcraft online game and, 14
companies. *See* organizations
construal, 156, 157, 158, 162–163
Creative Capital program, Dealogic, 101–104, 105–107, 111, 126
creativity
    best-self expression and, 60, 65
    Dealogic design team example of, 97–104, 105–107
    employees' class system affecting, 127
    experimentation and, 97–114
    finding balance between operational frame and freedom for, 45
    food delivery service example of, 127–134, 135–136

humble leadership's activation
of, 127
leadership potential affected by
expressions of, 43
as leadership trait for success, 42
managers' need to control employees and limits on, 41, 42, 43
seeking system's prompting of,
23, 104
Shell Oil's GameChanger program and, 107–112
team collaboration and, 74
uncertainty and negative bias
toward, 42–43, 89
Crossing the Unknown Sea
(Whyte), 65
curiosity
experimentation and, 86, 88
leader's prompting of, 123
learning situation and, 90, 101, 157
seeking system and, 17, 18, 37,
40, 74, 95
customer service
best-self activation and creativity
and, 60
Chinese bank branch example of,
117–123
food delivery service example of,
127–134, 135–136
KLM employees' use of social
media as example of, 45–49
role-playing exercises for, 120
UK food delivery business
example of, 127–132
SAS example of immersive client
experience policy and, 165–167
Wipro's individualized onboarding approach and, 54, 58

Dealogic design team, 97–104,
105–107
decision making, by teams, 75, 80
Deloitte, 3
depressive symptoms, 8, 31, 66
diversity, on teams, 75
dopamine
animating effect of, 23, 37
learning new things and release
of, 18, 24, 91
meaningful work and release of,
15, 24, 50, 95
negative work experiences and
shutting off of, 31, 38
purpose and release of, 141
seeking system and, 6, 17, 18, 24,
50, 95
time perception and, 15, 18
Drucker, Peter, 63
Dutcher, Janine, 61

Edmondson, Amy, 70, 89–90, 100,
101
Ely, Robin, 75
emotional systems, 16–17, 87
emotions
change and, 134
feeling sense of purpose and,
147–148, 149–151
narratives about purpose and,
160–161, 165
employees
affirming unique strengths of,
76–77
current conditions and need for
new way of working by, 8–9,
43–44

employees (*continued*)
  experience of lack of meaningful
    work by, 4–6
  feeling of anticipation and zest
    of, 18
  Industrial Revolution and organi-
    zational changes affecting, 7
  job titles of (*see* job titles)
  leaders' learning from, 123,
    124–125
  management practices for con-
    trol of, 7–8, 32–33, 40–44
  need for contributing vitality of,
    65–66
  scientific management's ap-
    proach to, 8, 32, 35–36, 37, 41
  specialized roles of, 37–40, 84–85
  tendency to disengage from
    tedious activities and, 8
  See also work environment
engagement
  feeling of purpose and, 143
  specialized roles of employees
    and lack of, 40
  surveys reporting lack of, 4, 6
  World of Warcraft online game as
    example of, 11–13
enthusiasm
  Dealogic design team project
    and, 99, 104, 105, 108–109
  experimenting and, 104
  feeling of purpose and, 142
  leaders' creation of, 94–95, 118,
    121, 122
  triggering employees' seeking
    systems for, 10, 14, 95
eudemonic happiness, 24–25
eudemonic well-being, 25

experimentation, 81–136
  bureaucratic leadership and
    stifling of, 124
  change seen as chance for, 89–90
  Creative Capital program's free
    time for, 101–104, 105–107
  curiosity and, 88
  Dealogic design team example
    of, 97–104, 105–107
  employees' commitment to work
    after, 95–96, 121
  employees' desire to try new
    ideas during, 91–94
  finding balance between opera-
    tional frame and freedom for,
    45, 87, 112–114, 121
  freedom and creativity and,
    97–114
  Google's "20 percent time" policy
    and, 112–113
  improving employees' enthusi-
    asm for, 14
  Italian example of lean manu-
    facturing and team's use of
    learning and, 83–84, 88, 90,
    91–94, 95–96
  keeping momentum going in,
    105–107
  KLM employees' use of social
    media as example of, 45–49
  leaders' creating of employee
    enthusiasm and, 94–95,
    135–136
  leadership and, 115–136
  leaders' openness to employees'
    suggestions about, 120–122
  learning goals in innovation and,
    100–101

managers' encouragement of, 90–92

managers' need to control employees and limits on, 41, 42

organization's suppression of, 7

ownership of vision and, 93

play and, 87, 88, 90, 96, 105, 106

safe zones for, 87–88, 93

seeking systems and, 14, 16, 24, 49, 95, 96, 104, 135–136

serious play and, 83–96

Shell Oil's GameChanger program and, 107–112

specialized roles of employees and lack of, 40

Standard Chartered Bank branch visit example of leader's approach to, 115–123, 135–136

team collaboration and, 74

World of Warcraft online game as example of, 15

exploration

  managers' need to control employees and limits on, 41

  organization's suppression of, 7

  seeking system's prompting of, 6, 22–24, 26, 27

  specialized roles of employees and lack of, 40

extrinsic motivation, 88, 99, 142

Facebook

  KLM employees' use of, 46–49

  self-expression using, 77

fear system, 33–37

  bureaucratic leadership and, 124

  impact on employees of, 8

inhibiting relationship between seeking system and, 35, 41

management's use of, 35–37

organizations' activation of, 8

performance and, 19, 20

play experiment with rats illustrating, 34–35

survival and evolutionary use of, 33–34

feeling alive

  leader's purpose for helping employees with, 173

  organizational life preventing, 4

  seeking system activation and, 7, 42, 136

  signature strengths and, 66

food delivery service example of leadership, 127–134, 135–136

Ford, Henry, 32, 36

Fredrickson, Barbara, 26

Fruitema, Marnix, 47

Gallup Institute, 76–77

Gallup polls, 4, 6

GameChanger program, Shell Oil, 107–112

Garrelfs, Rick, 153–154

Goddard, Jules, 43–44

Goodnight, James, 165–166, 167

Google, "20 percent time" policy at, 101, 112–113

Graham, Terri Funk, 10

Grant, Adam, 67–68, 69, 72, 145–147, 148, 149, 150

Greer, Lindy, 73–74

Haddon, Toby, 99–101, 104, 105
Hamel, Gary, 118
happiness
  health related to, 25–27
  hedonic versus eudemonic, 24–25
  quick quiz on experience of, 25
  seeking system and, 24–27
  using unique strengths and, 76
Wipro employees' writing exercise
    on experience of best self and,
    54–56
Happy (Brown), 27
Harari, Yuval Noah, 40
Harvard Kennedy School of Gov-
    ernment, 64–65
health
  employees' sense of purpose and,
    141, 173
  learned helplessness's impact
    on, 100
  purposeful happiness and, 25–26,
    141
  seeking system related to, 25–27,
    141
  stories we tell ourselves about,
    162–163
hedonic happiness, 24, 25, 26
Hekman, David, 123, 132
helplessness. *See* learned
  helplessness
Hoffmann, Dave, 146, 147
Hoffmann-La Roche AG, 148–150
humble leadership, 123–127
  benefits of, 126–127
  huddles with employees used in,
    117, 118–119, 120
  learning from employees in, 123,
    124–125

seeking systems and, 127
Standard Chartered Bank branch
    visits as example of, 115–123

IBM, 42
identities
  best selves stories revealing, 60
  job titles reflecting, 68, 69–70, 72,
    74–75
  team members and, 74–75
Ikram, Irfan, 105, 106
immune system
  purposeful happiness and, 26
  relational best-self activation
    and, 63
incentives, 7, 142, 144, 146
Industrial Revolution, 7, 8, 76, 126
innovation
  change and organization's need
    for, 9
  Dealogic's Creative Capital pro-
    gram for, 101–104, 105–107
  finding balance between opera-
    tional frame and freedom for,
    45
  humans' biological wiring for,
    135
  improving employees' enthusi-
    asm for, 14
  leaders' nurturing of culture of,
    104, 105
  learning goals versus perfor-
    mance outcomes in, 100–101
  managers' need to control em-
    ployees and lack of, 41, 42, 43
  seeking system's prompting of,
    23, 24

Shell Oil's GameChanger program and, 107–112
uncertainty and negative bias toward, 42–43, 89
intrinsic motivation, 66, 78, 88, 99, 104, 107, 121, 142, 161, 167

job titles
common themes in use of, 69–72
Disneyland's use of, 68
focus on purpose using, 73, 142
individual self-expression and, 68–73
leaders' encouragement of, 79
Make-a-Wish Foundation's use of, 67–73, 142
organizations' encouraging employee customization of, 79–80
personal identities inside organization and, 69–70
personal identities outside organization and, 72
psychological safety and, 70–71
seeking system and, 73
team functioning and, 73–75
Wipro's onboarding and, 50

key performance indicators (KPIs), 44, 99, 100, 108, 123
KLM, 45–49, 126
Koning, Lisette Ebeling, 47

Laitenen, Janne, 140
leaders
authority of, 118, 128

best selves approach for activating seeking system and, 65–66
bureaucratic approach to, 32, 124
emperor versus facilitator roles of, 119–120
employees' suggestions about experiments and, 120–122
enthusiasm created by, 94–95, 118, 121, 122
experimentation and, 115–136
food delivery service example of, 127–134, 135–136
huddles with employees used in, 117, 118–119, 120
humble leadership approach to, 123–127
innovation culture nurtured by, 104, 105
KLM employees' use of social media and, 47–48
learning from employees by, 123, 124–125
personal messages about purpose from, 146–147, 148, 155
power used by, 124, 126
purpose for leading and, 172–173
relational self-affirmation training of, 64–65
seeking systems activated by, 119, 120, 122
self-expression encouraged by, 119, 134
self-expression organizations and mindset of, 79
Standard Chartered Bank branch visit example of, 115–123, 135–136

leaders (*continued*)
  tactics in sharing purpose with
    employees used by, 148–151
  triggers of seeking system used
    by, 49–50
  See also managers
lean manufacturing, 84–86, 90–94,
  95–96, 110
learned helplessness
  arrogance as form of, 125
  employees' reaction to, 100, 108,
    127
  fear-based management and, 35
  human impact of, 30–31
  managers' attempts to change,
    127, 132, 136
  Seligman's dog experiment on,
    29–30, 124–125
learning
  bureaucratic leadership and
    stifling of, 124
  change seen as chance for,
    89–90
  experimental safe zones for,
    87–88, 93
  improving employees' enthusi-
    asm for, 14
  innovation and, 100–101
  KLM employees' use of social
    media as example of, 46–49
  leaders' prompting of, 123, 124,
    125–126, 129
  leaders' role-playing to model,
    130–131
  managers' encouragement of,
    90–92
  organization's suppression of, 7
  play and, 96

seeking system and impulse for,
  6, 24, 26, 40, 91, 135
Shell Oil's GameChanger program and, 111
specialized roles of employees
  and lack of, 38, 40
learning-playing sequence, 86
Lee, Julia, 63
Lerch, Susan Fenters, 68, 71
liking system, 23

Make-a-Wish Foundation, 67–73,
  142
management practices
  fear used in, 35–37
  Google's "20 percent time" policy
    and, 101, 112–113
  need for control of employees
    using, 7–8, 31–33, 40–44, 77–78
  strengths-based, 76–77
managers
  best selves approach and em-
    ployee interactions with, 60
  control of employees by, 40–42,
    43
  employees' creativity and, 43
  employees' experimentation
    and learning encouraged by,
    90–92
  older assumptions and practices
    used by, 43–44
  See also leaders
Mann, Jeffrey, 46
Maslow, Abraham, 23–24
meaning
  happiness and sense of, 25
  job titles and, 70

manager's engagement with
employees' sense of, 134
seeking system and exploring for,
6, 26
meaningful work, employee's
experience of lack of, 4–6
medical teams, learning new procedures by, 89–90
Mertens, Bert, 154
Microsoft, 167–170
Milkman, Katherine, 162–163
Min, Zhang, 115–118
motivation
creativity and, 88, 104
employee's experience of lack of, 4
experimental safe zones and, 88
feeling of purpose and, 142
intrinsic versus extrinsic, 88, 99,
142
leaders and, 123
learned helplessness and, 30
scientific management and,
32–33, 41
seeking system's enhancement
of, 7, 21–24, 104
triggering employees' seeking
systems and, 10
work similar to "real life" and, 66
Mueller, Jennifer, 42–43
My Life as Night Elf Priest
(Nardi), 11

Nadella, Satya, 168
Nardi, Bonnie, 11–14, 15, 16, 23, 91
narratives about purpose, 153–173
dealing with chemotherapy examples of, 159–161

depth of meaning in, 162–165
emotions and, 160–161, 165
employee's personal interpretation of, 155–158
level of construal in constructing,
156, 157, 158, 162–163
Microsoft example of client
involvement and, 167–170
Rabobank example of communicating, 153–155
reasons for choosing and reframing, 158–161
SAS example of immersive
client experience policy and,
165–167
seeking system activation and,
170–171
neurotransmitters. *See* dopamine
Nietzsche, Friedrich, 163
Nokian Tyres, 139–412, 165
Novant Health, 72–73

onboarding sessions
employees' need to fit in and be
accepted and, 56
experiment comparing approaches used in, 57–58
organization's traditional approach to, 56–57
Wipro's best selves exercise
during, 53–56, 57, 58, 60
organizations
best selves and employee's distinctive identity in, 60
current conditions and need for
new way of working by, 8–9,
43–44

organizations (*continued*)
  experience of lack of meaningful
    work in, 4–6
  finding balance between oper-
    ational frame and employee
    freedom in, 44–45
  Industrial Revolution and chang-
    es to, 7
  job titles in (*see* job titles)
  management practices for
    control of employees in, 7–8,
    31–33, 40–44, 77–78
  need for contributing vitality of
    all employees in, 65–66
  onboarding sessions used by,
    56–57
  seeking system's suppression by,
    3–8
  as self-expression vehicles, 76–80
  specialized roles and standard-
    ized processes in, 37–40, 84–85
  strengths-based management
    techniques in, 76–77
  See also work environment
Owens, Bradley, 123, 132

Page, Larry, 112, 113
Panksepp, Jaak, 8, 17, 34, 35, 87
performance, employee
  best-self activation and, 57, 58,
    60–61, 65
  forced-ranking approach to, 78
  learning goals and improvements
    in, 101
  seeking system and, 18–21, 146
  servant-oriented leadership and,
    126

  signature strengths and, 66
  small changes by managers
    affecting, 122, 145
  strengths-based management
    techniques and, 77
performance, team
  diversity and, 75
  self-expression and, 63–65, 75
  servant-oriented leadership and,
    126
performance metrics, 5, 7, 40, 42,
  44, 78, 99–100
performance situations, and
  anxiety, 19, 20, 90, 99–101,
  128, 144
play
  experimentation and, 87, 88, 90,
    96, 105, 106
  fear system's inhibition of, 34–35,
    41
  managers' need to control em-
    ployees and limits on, 41
  seeking system stimulation by,
    87, 96
  teamwork with, 74, 75
Polzer, Jeffrey, 75
power, leaders' use of, 124, 126
problem solving ability, 20, 21,
  63
  creativity and, 43
  experimenting with new ways
    of, 95
  older management assumptions
    and practices working against,
    44
psychological safety, 70–71
purpose, 137–173
  creating, 143–144

emotional aspect of feeling sense
of, 147–148, 149–151, 160–161,
165

employee's health and longevity
affected by sense of, 141, 173

employee's personal interpretation of, 155–158

experiencing impact of work
and, 49, 139–151

experimentation and, 123

happiness related to, 25–26, 141

job titles reflecting, 73, 142

leaders' finding of their own,
172–173

leader's personal messages
about, 146–147, 148, 155

Microsoft example of client
involvement and, 167–170

motivation and, 123

narratives about, 153–173

Nokian Tyres example of,
139–142, 165

onboarding sessions and, 57

Rabobank example of communicating, 153–155

Roche example of leaders' tactics, 148–151

SAS example of immersive client
experience policy and, 165–167

seeking system and, 16, 142–43,
144, 146, 147, 149, 150, 155,
164–165, 166–167, 170–171

as trigger for seeking system,
14, 16

World of Warcraft online game as
example of, 16

purposeful happiness, 25–26, 141

PwC, 128, 130–131, 133

Rabobank, 153–155

Rastogi, Amit, 60

rewards
employee motivation and, 21, 41,
99, 107, 123, 125, 134

seeking system versus, 22, 23, 24

Rigoni, Brandon, 76–77

Ritz, Dorothee, 168–170

Roberts, Laura, 59, 61

Roche, 148–150

role-playing
customer service using, 120

manager education using,
130–131

safe zones, 87–88, 93

SAS Industries, 165–167

scientific management
employee control in, 8, 32, 35–36,
37, 114

seeking system under, 41–42

seeking systems, 1–50
activating a life more worth
living and, 76

animating effect of, 23–24

balance between operational
frame and employee freedom
for activating, 45

benefits of, 16–27

best selves approach for activating, 61, 65–66

brain location of, 6, 17, 23, 24,
26, 135

description of behavior motivated by, 6–7

dopamine release and, 6, 17, 18,
24, 50, 95

seeking systems (*continued*)
experimental safe zones for activating, 87–88
experimentation as trigger for, 15
fear system's inhibiting relationship with, 35, 41
feeling of anticipation and zest from, 18
gaming and, 161
happiness and health and, 24–27
how it works, 17–18
humble leadership's activation of, 127
leaders' use of triggers of, 49–50
learning and activation of, 91
learning environment and, 6, 24, 26, 40, 91
management's need to control employees and, 31–33, 41
managers' encouragement of employees' experimentation and, 90–91, 132
motivation enhanced by, 21–24
negative work experiences and shutting off of, 31
online games and, 13–14
organizations' need for new way of working by activating, 8–9, 36–37
organizations' suppression of, 3–8
performance enhanced by, 18–21
play and stimulation of, 87, 96
proactive approach of employees and, 36–37
purpose as trigger for, 16
rewards versus, 23
scientific management's impact on, 41–42

self-expression as trigger for, 14–15
self-expression organizations activating, 78–79
self-reflective titles and, 73
social networks for activating, 63, 64
specialized roles of employees and impact on, 38–40
stories about work and, 164–165
team collaboration and, 74
team diversity and, 75
three triggers for activating, 14–16
work environments and, 114
World of Warcraft online game and active participation of, 11–14
self-actualization
benefits of, 63
long-term cascading effects of, 60
Maslow's ideas about, 23–24
social networks and, 63, 64
team functioning and, 64–65
as trigger of seeking system, 63
self-affirmation, 61, 64, 69, 76, 79
self-expression, 51–80
best selves at work and, 53–66
employee enthusiasm and, 49, 119
experiment comparing onboarding approaches using, 57–58
feeling like ourselves at work and, 59–60
finding balance between operational frame and freedom for, 45
KLM employees' use of social media as example of, 49

leader's encouragement of, 119, 134

Make-a-Wish Foundation's use of job titles and, 67–73

manager's engagement with employees' desire for, 134

organizations as vehicles for, 76–80

promoting, 67–80

teams and, 63–65, 80

as trigger for seeking system, 14, 16

Wipro's onboarding exercise using, 53–56, 57, 58, 60

World of Warcraft online game as example of, 14–15

Seligman, Martin, 18, 29, 66

sense of purpose. *See* purpose

Shell Oil's GameChanger program, 107–112

signature strengths, 63, 66

SMART goals, 44, 144

social media

KLM employees' use of, 46–49

self-expression using, 77

social networks, relational best-self activations from, 62–63, 64

specialization, 37–40, 44, 84–85

Standard Chartered Bank, China, 115–123, 124, 126, 135–136

standardization, 7, 37, 44

Stoic philosophy, 27

storytelling, in product development, 110

stress responses

best-self activation and, 60, 63

fun job titles and, 71

play and, 87

positive emotions and, 20

seeking system and, 19

team learning-playing sequence and, 86

Swann, William, 75

Taylor, Frederick, 32, 35, 41

teams

change seen as chance for experimentation and learning by, 89–90

creativity example and Dealogic design team, 97–104, 105–107

diversity on, 75

employees' sense of purpose and, 16

Google's "20 percent time" policy and productivity of, 112–113

Italian example of lean manufacturing and learning by, 83–84, 88, 90, 91–94, 95–96

relational self-affirmation training for leaders of, 64–65

seeking systems and, 75

self-expression by members of, 63–65, 80

triggering employees' seeking systems and capabilities for, 10

World of Warcraft online role-playing game and, 11–13, 14

Thomas, David, 75

3M, 101

time perception, and dopamine, 15, 18

titles. *See* job titles

training, in lean manufacturing, 85–86

Trapp, Antony, 102–103, 104, 105
"20 percent time" policy (Google),
    101, 112–113

Valve Software, 44–45
Vandewalle, Don, 100–01
vision, experimentation and owner-
    ship of, 93

wanting system, 23
Wardley, Duncan, 128, 130, 131, 133,
    134
Warren, Tim, 107–108, 109–110
Whyte, Davd, 65, 66
Wipro onboarding sessions
    experiment comparing tradition-
        al approaches with, 57–58
    individualized approach to,
        53–56, 57, 58, 60
wise intervention
    benefits of using, 59–60
    food delivery service example of,
        132, 133
    Wipro's individualized onboard-
        ing approach as, 58–59
work environment
    animating effect of seeking sys-
        tem and, 23–24

current conditions and need for
    new way of working in, 8–9
employees' lack of involvement
    in or enthusiasm for job and,
    3–4
example of lack of meaningful
    work and not being best self
    in, 4–6
feeling of anticipation and zest
    in, 18
finding balance between oper-
    ational frame and employee
    freedom in, 44–45
job titles and (*see* job titles)
management practices for
    control of employees in, 7–8,
    31–33, 40–44, 77–78
scientific management and
    standardization in, 8, 32, 35–36,
    37, 41
seeking systems and, 114
specialized roles and standard-
    ized processes in, 37–40,
    84–85
tendency to disengage from
    tedious activities in, 8
workers. *See* employees
World of Warcraft, 11–14, 23,
    77, 91
Wright, Jason, 87

ACKNOWLEDGMENTS

This book would not have been possible without the support of my family. Thank you Alison for your love and for making life stable enough to write a book. And thank you Mom and Dad for giving me my education and for encouraging me to try new directions.

Thank you Adam Grant, who helped me with this book writing and publishing process.

Thank you Tim Sullivan, Kevin Evers, and the Harvard Business Review Press team who helped me craft and shape the book.

Thank you to Ingrid Wills, John Wills, and all the fine folks at Essentic who have invested so much in the research over the years.

Finally, I want to acknowledge all the executives and MBAs who have helped me understand engagement at work, and how much better work and life can feel when the seeking system is activated.

ABOUT THE AUTHOR

DAN CABLE is Professor of Organisational Behaviour at London Business School. Dan's research and teaching focus on employee engagement, change, organizational culture, leadership mindset, and the linkage between brands and employee behaviors.

Dan's first book was *Change to Strange: Create a Great Organization by Building a Strange Workforce,* and he has published two edited books and more than fifty articles in top scientific journals. His most recent research was published in *Harvard Business Review, Sloan Management Review,* the *Academy of Management Journal,* and *Administrative Science Quarterly.* This research has been featured in the *Economist, Financial Times, Wall Street Journal, CNBC, New York Times,* and *Businessweek.* The Academy of Management has twice honored Dan with "Best article" awards, and the *Academy of Management Perspectives* ranked Dan among the "Top 25 most influential management scholars."

Dan has worked with a broad range of organizations ranging from high-tech startups to the World Economic Forum. His recent clients include Carlsberg, Coca Cola, EY, Goldman Sachs, HSBC, Ikea, McDonalds, MS Amlin, Prudential, PwC, Rabobank, Roche, Siemens, and Twitter.